Praise for *The Way of Being Lost* by Victoria Price

The Way of Being Lost is a beautifully written story of one woman's journey of healing to stand in the fullness of life that calls to us all. Joy is big medicine, and when Victoria Price decided to follow it wherever it would lead her, she embarked on the heroine's journey to her true self. May her courage to follow what is true inspire you to release the stories that were never yours and rekindle the courage to claim your truth."

> —**Gail Larsen**, teacher and author of
> *Transformational Speaking*

The Way of Being Lost reminds us that the path to finding one's self can be the result of first being lost. A poignant story by the privileged daughter of a Hollywood icon reflecting back on a life spent lost but realizing life's greatest lessons often occur when one doesn't know where they are going."

> —**James R. Doty, M.D.**, *New York Times* bestselling author
> of *Into the Magic Shop*

"Victoria Price's journey is a truly inspiring one. She looks both outward and inward to find joy all around her. She has been a close friend to me for years and I have always been moved by her story and thrilled that she is finally sharing it with the world."

> —**Melissa Etheridge**, Grammy and Oscar-winning musician
> and activist

"In *The Way of Being Lost*, Victoria does what all of us wish to do—seeks out her own relationship with spirituality and makes the sacred a part of her everyday life, merely by observing the world around us in all its glory. Her writing shows the struggles of this way of being, but also its rewards."

—**Miranda MacPherson**, author of
Meditations on Boundless Love

"Victoria Price is a fighter—for her belief in a world that is connected by Love, and for her own connection to Joy. Her commitment to living as her truest self is an inspiration for us all—match point, Ms. Price."

—**Martina Navratilova**, tennis player, activist, wife, parent, and author of *Shape Your Self* and other books

"Victoria Price has written a book that will ignite your soul. With remarkable bravery she shares her story—warts and all—of healing financial and emotional wounds through the daily practice of joy. Victoria's core message that it's never too late to fix old habits that no longer serve us is delivered in such a raw and intimate way that you can't help but be inspired to embark upon your own journey to joy."

—**Manisha Thakor**, founder, MoneyZen Financial Education

"Victoria Price boldly faces down the false lessons around money (and more) that she imbibed from an early age in this honest, relatable memoir. She comes out on the other side liberated from a desire to accumulate endlessly, embracing her own values instead of living by the standards of others. It's an inspiring journey to freedom that we can all relate to."

—**Kate Levinson**, author of *Emotional Currency*

"Victoria Price writes beautifully of our need to forgive ourselves and others if we truly want to find happiness. Her journey through forgiveness and love shines with hard-earned wisdom, which she shares as a generous offering of her broken-open heart."

—**Diane Berke**, founder and spiritual director,
One Spirit Learning Alliance

"The truest pilgrims are those who become so lost along the way that it takes a miracle or an angel to bring them to altar of their innermost heart's desire. Victoria Price's stirring memoir offers us the truest of all pilgrimage maps—the one that makes sense of the present by following highways and byways, the trails and barely discernible footpaths of the past, showing that all of it was necessary . . . all was as it should be . . . everything was blessed."

—**Clark Strand**, author of *Waking Up to the Dark*

"Intimate and brave, this wise memoir invites us to reexamine what we really want from our own lives—and empowers us, too, with real tools for reaching for the joy we all deserve."

—**Perdita Finn**, co-author of *The Reluctant Psychic*

"In this spirited, spiritual exploration of her own life and those of her famous parents—one joyous, one terrified—Victoria Price shows us with sword-sharp self-awareness how to face down our fears to find those happy true selves who have been waiting unseen inside us for gosh-knows-how-long."

—**Anneli Rufus**, author of *Unworthy: How to Stop Hating Yourself*; *Stuck: Why We Can't (or Won't) Move On*; *Party of One: The Loners' Manifesto*; and more

THE WAY OF BEING LOST

A ROAD TRIP TO MY TRUEST SELF

THE WAY OF BEING LOST

A ROAD TRIP TO MY TRUEST SELF

VICTORIA PRICE

ixia
PRESS

Mineola, New York

Bibliographical Note

The Way of Being Lost: A Road Trip to My Truest Self
is a new work, first published by Ixia Press in 2018.

International Standard Book Number

ISBN-13: 978-0-486-81605-0
ISBN-10: 0-486-81605-2

IXIA PRESS
An imprint of Dover Publications, Inc.

Manufactured in the United States by LSC Communications
81605201   2017
www.doverpublications.com/ixiapress

To the three Marys:
In gratitude, healing, and joy.

CONTENTS

CONTENTS

CUTTING LOOSE

Sometimes from sorrow, for no reason,
you sing. For no reason,
you accept
the way of being lost, cutting loose
from all else and electing
a world
where you go where you want to.

Arbitrary, a sound comes, a
reminder
that a steady center is holding
all else. If you listen, that
sound
will tell you where it is and you
can slide your way past
trouble.

Certain twisted monsters
always bar the path—but that's
when
you get going best, glad to be lost,
learning how real it is
here
on earth, again and again.

—William Stafford

THE ME IN THE MIRROR

One month before my 49th birthday, standing in front of the mirror in the tasteful dark slate-grey bathroom of my Santa Fe home, I heard myself say:

You're doing everything right.

You're in a long-term relationship with a wonderful person.

You live in a beautiful house in a city you love.

You've gone a long way toward getting out of debt.

You've begun a new career and already made a name for yourself.

You've climbed out of a huge hole and pulled your life together.

You did it!

And you're miserable.

I stared at myself in the mirror for a full minute, looking myself in the eye. I couldn't argue. I *had* already accomplished almost everything I had set out to do when my life had fallen apart five years earlier and I lost my home, gave up most of my material possessions, and found myself millions of dollars in debt.

Since then, my new career as a designer had taken off. My reinvented art gallery / design studio / lifestyle store had survived the recent Great Recession and was finally rebounding. I had paid off a huge amount of what I owed. I had a kind and loving partner, the best dog in the world, and we were renting a lovely home in a city where I'd felt privileged to live for more than two decades. I had even begun to face down the suicidal shame and depression I had felt about all my financial losses. Now I was embarking on a year that promised great excitement—lots of travel and big design projects.

But what that urgent inner voice had said was true. I could no longer deny or ignore it. I *was* miserable.

I looked at myself in the mirror and said out loud, "If I have to keep living like this for another 40 years, I won't make it."

That realization hit me like a punch in the gut—and that wasn't the half of it. What terrified me even more was that this conversation I was having with myself at almost 50 was just a variation on the same conversation I had had at almost 40, and at almost 30 before that. Imagining myself having that same conversation with myself at almost 60 was more than I could bear.

Each decade I had asked myself all the big questions we all ask ourselves:

Why am I here?
What am I meant to be doing?
How can I help the world?

Each decade I vowed to find those answers.
Each decade I failed.

This time my big questions felt far more urgent:

Why have I never felt like my truest self?
What keeps stopping me from living my best life?
What would that life look like anyway?
And how can living that life make the world a better place?

After almost 50 years on the planet, I felt like I had done nothing that had really mattered.

In that moment, I promised myself that I would change my life.

When Things Fall Apart

For the next nine months of 2011, I clung to that promise like a lifeline. I said the same thing over and over again to myself, and to anyone else who would listen: I refuse to look myself in the mirror ten years from now and still feel like I have never shown up to my own life. I have to find a way to do something that makes a difference to someone other than me.

I meant it.

There was only one small problem. I had no idea *how* to change my life. I just hoped that if I kept learning to listen to myself and put one foot in front of the other, my new life would fall into place.

If it had been that simple, I wouldn't have written this book.

When I invited the still, small voice that had spoken truth back into my life, I asked it to take me where I needed to be led.

It did.

While it was doing that, it also tore my whole life as I knew it apart.

I began 2012 by leaving my six-year relationship. The guilt I initially felt about walking away from someone I truly loved almost derailed my whole journey. Ultimately, however, leaving my partner to start a new relationship with myself became my third rail, the juice that kept me on the track of my truth. The only way I could truly honor our breakup was to keep changing my life.

Risking that first big change inevitably led to risking another. Then another, and another. After my breakup I moved from the charming home we had been renting out in the country into a quirky space in the Santa Fe barrio. Next I downsized my retail store. Two years later, I closed it altogether. This meant not only letting go of loyal long-term employees, but also walking away from a business I had spent more than a decade building. I began co-creating a different entrepreneurial model with new investment partners. This required that I spend less and less time at home with my dog, my friends, and my colleagues in Santa Fe and more and more time alone on the road piecing together a patchwork-quilt career of interior design intermingled with public speaking and appearances.

Each change brought both freedom and fear. While I reveled in new opportunities to build a life filled with creative conversations and inspiring connections, I often found myself wanting to turn back and run for the safety of familiar places and people and behaviors: A romantic relationship. A steady job with a regular paycheck. A big life in a small town surrounded by people I knew. Yet every time I succumbed to the siren call of supposed comfort, that wise inner voice urged me on.

Stay true to you, it said to me. *Even if you don't quite trust who you are yet.*

Although every one step forward usually felt accompanied by many more steps back, I remained committed to all this change. At some point, however, it began to feel like all I was doing was playing 52-card pickup with my life.

That's when it hit me. I had been making all of these changes in order to keep my promise to show up to myself. Yet I was no less miserable than I had been before. How could that be?

I needed to find some answers to some very tough questions:

Was I just changing for change's sake?
Was all this transformation helping or hurting me—and others?
Could I trust this still, small voice leading me?
Whose voice was it even?
And why was I still so miserable?

Just a few years after that conversation with myself in the mirror, I found myself at another major crossroads. I had been so eager to tear my former life down to the studs in order to rebuild it. Now my new life didn't feel much different than the old one. More like a fresh hell. A replacement misery.

Unwilling to tuck tail and turn back, once again I had to find a new way forward.

~

It is said that the longest journey any of us can take is from our heads to our hearts. For those of us whose controlling minds feel like our security blankets, this can feel more like a knock-down, drag-out battle than a pleasant country drive—the voices in our heads waging nuclear war with the inner knowing of our hearts.

In that moment in the mirror, I let myself hear the call of my own heart for the first time in decades. But in the years that followed, I reverted to listening to all the big opinions I had accumulated in my head, which felt far more familiar than the heart-based voice of truth I had spent a lifetime learning to ignore.

This happens to us all. We are taught to value the voices of our elders, our superiors, and our idols more than we trust our own deep and fundamental discerning. Even the messages in books, television, movies, newspapers, and magazines can seem more real than our inner wisdom.

Thomas Merton called these the voices of our false and true selves. "Every one of us is shadowed by an illusory person: a false self," Merton wrote. The problem, he says, is that none of us is "very good at recognizing illusions, least of all the ones we cherish about the superficial, external self which we commonly identify with the first person singular. Our reality, our true self, is hidden."

This true self is who we have always been—under all of the shoulds and rules, behaviors and lifestyles in which we are all taught to put our faith throughout our lives. This self has been drowned out by the voices of everyone we are supposed to obey, emulate, and admire—our parents, teachers, peers, bosses, spouses, lovers, and partners.

In order to really transform my life, then, I had to invite my true self out of hiding and into the light and then learn to hear her voice.

When I promised to change my life, I had set off in search of an imagined future to be lived by the person I hoped to become. Still guided by my old stories, I ended up driving around and around in circles because I had been calibrating my compass to a false north. Now I had to learn to trust the inner GPS of my heart, which is always guided by Love.

I knew that learning to do that would be no easy task. But I was motivated. If I turned around, I would only end up right where I had begun. Exactly nowhere. That's where following my old familiar maps had ultimately gotten me. Nowhere.

I had to keep asking the hard questions that would help me align with my true self. Questions like—Why had I stopped listening to her in the first place? And where had she been all that time I'd been listening to the voices of others?

She had never gone anywhere. She had never stopped speaking true. It was just that each time I had elected to listen to the world's supposed wisdom instead, I created another brick in a wall that had come to block her voice. A wall that had gotten thicker and thicker, until it finally became soundproof.

Over time, I had almost forgotten that I even had a true self because I could no longer hear her. All those outside voices had come to feel like "me."

By inviting my true self back into my life, the very existence of my small false self felt threatened. As she watched me make change after change, she realized that if she didn't do something, she might end up chucked out on the curb with everything else I had been willing to lose. So she started kicking and screaming, doing everything she could to get my attention, holding on for dear life. My old self was not going down without a fight.

That's when I suddenly realized that what felt like anxiety about all these changes was actually not "my" anxiety at all. It was the telltale heart of my old familiar self, beating in terror of being buried alive underneath the floorboards of my new life. That fearful small self, panicked at losing its hold over me, was actually the only "me" that *could* feel miserable.

Although all the old voices in my head were raising a ruckus, those voices weren't me. They never had been. That was why I never felt like I had shown up to my own life or contributed something meaningful to the world: I had been playacting a part in the script my false self had been writing for me.

The only real person any of us can be is our true self. Only by living as our truest selves can we show up to the lives we are meant to be living. The language of this self is Love. *That,* I realized, is what I could trust. As I began to learn to listen to my heart instead of my head, every time I heard lack or fear I would know it wasn't true. The more I listened to the loving voice of my true self, the more that old familiar misery would fade back into its native nothingness. But how could I learn to tune out fear and hear Love instead?

Although my old familiar self had developed a lot of job security, I had one ace in the hole. Just as a parasite needs a host body, our false selves cannot exist unless we ask them in to set up shop in our subconscious. By identifying the stories my false self had created and then dismantling them, I could step into the authentic life of my true self at last.

⌒

This brought me to my next big question: Why now? Why had it taken me so long to listen to that still, small loving voice of the real me? Why hadn't the epiphany that led me to start changing my life come at 29, or 39, or even when I hit what most people would have called my "bottom"? Instead, it came five years *after* going through a series of financial and personal disasters, which felt like one of those made-for-TV movie plots that seem completely unbelievable . . . until they happen to you. It took me a while to see that it had taken everything falling apart and then getting mostly put back together for me to finally hear my own wake-up call.

I know now that when things fall apart, sometimes all we can do is go into crisis mode and begin to pick up the pieces, suture the wounds, and do damage control. Pema Chödrön wrote a whole book about what happens when things fall apart, a book I had picked up from time to occasional time, glanced through, and then actively avoided—like cleaning the toilet or sorting my tax papers. I wasn't raised to stay in the place where things fall apart. I was raised to pull myself together and get on with it.

It has taken me a long time to truly understand Pema Chödrön's teaching: "We think that the point is to pass the test or overcome the problem, but the truth is that things don't really get solved. They come together and they fall apart. Then they come together again and fall apart again. It's just like that. The healing comes from letting there be room for all of this to happen: room for grief, for relief, for misery, for joy."

Six years earlier, when my whole life had begun to unravel at the seams, then crashed and burned, before it finally drowned at sea, I never allowed myself the room for grief, relief, misery, or joy.

Shame, on the other hand—I had plenty of that.

Shame screamed at me:

You had no idea what you were doing when you made that business deal. You're not a business person. What were you thinking?

You should have saved more, spent less, not gotten in over your head.

You shouldn't have deluded yourself into thinking it would all work out one day.

Shame came in with a battering ram and hit me hard over and over again.

Guilt? I had loads of that, too.

All I could hear were some very old tapes in my head—the voices of my mother and my father berating me:

You were terrible with money as a child. Nothing's changed. You're still a financial disaster.

Now you've gone and lost everything we hoped you would have for yourself. How could you?

Guilt was the leaden albatross which I never took off my neck.

Grief, relief, misery, and joy, however, I quickly swept under the rug. Then I got straight to work putting the pieces of my life back together as though it had been a jigsaw puzzle, with only one right way back to wholeness.

It had never occurred to me that the life I had been living had fallen apart so that I could finally see just how broken it had always been.

My parents would both probably say that the best gift my mother ever bought my dad was an ancient black Etruscan pot that she found when they were in Rome. It had been mended once, absolutely meticulously, so that you had to look very, very closely to see the hairline cracks that attested to its imperfection. My father, who rarely saw a pot he did not covet, naturally loved it. But what he loved even more than the ancient elegant ebony vessel itself was the beautiful job of the almost invisible reconstruction.

That would have been good enough.

It got better.

When they packed everything to go home, as per usual for two omnivorous collectors, they had bought so many things that they were overflowing their checked and carry-on luggage. They had intended to carry the fragile pot on board with them, but they simply had too much to take. So my dad hit upon the idea of re-breaking the pot, piece by piece and then carefully reconstructing it when he got back home.

That's exactly what he did. For weeks after they got back from Rome, my mother would find my dad holed up in his study, Wilhold Glue in hand, putting that perfectly imperfect mended yet whole 2,500-year-old pot back together with painstaking care.

After things fell apart for me, I took my broken imperfect life and tried to reconstruct it just as my father had that black Etruscan pot—so meticulously, so perfectly, that only I would ever know how badly it had been broken and how many times. Which is to say, I took the image of the life I had had—which had been based on the image of what I thought my life was supposed to be, which had been based on everything I had been taught growing up—and I tried to rebuild that.

I worked harder than I had ever worked in order to assuage the almost unbearable guilt and shame I felt. I tried harder than I had ever tried to do anything to Humpty Dumpty myself back together again. Not understanding that everything had fallen apart in the first place—in fact had fallen apart over and over and over again—precisely because the life I had been trying to live for thirty years had never really been mine in the first place.

In retrospect, I now know that it was that futile effort which brought me to that life-altering conversation with myself in that mirror: To have worked so hard recreating someone else's idea of my life and then to still end up so miserable was my last straw.

Understanding that helped me see that my epiphany in the mirror and my subsequent decision to change my life were only a beginning. Even my promise to start listening to my true self was merely a tentative first step on a much longer path.

I had to become willing to break my own life into little pieces again—and again, and again—but *not* to rebuild another better pot from the shards of the old one. I had to dismantle my life so that I could see that pot had never really been me at all. Then— and this was what I really didn't want to hear for the longest time—I had to let the whole damn thing go. Not just the pot, but even the idea of the pot.

I really didn't like that plan.

Surely, I thought, I can keep just a few pretty pieces.

Just the ones I love the most . . .

Okay. Okay.

I get it.

I'll let those go, too.

How about another kind of pot?

A different color?

A newer one?

But whenever I wavered, that still, small voice of my true self let herself be heard: *That's not how this works.*

Slowly but surely, kicking and screaming much of the way, I began to get that I had to be willing to jettison all of the accumulated old stories—ideas, ideologies, identities—that I had come to call "me."

Having spent a lifetime trying to follow rules I never fully believed, doing what I had been taught, coloring (mostly) within the lines, *of course* this radical way of living felt wildly uncomfortable!

From the outside, I had always looked like an iconoclast, a creative free spirit. But underneath my own skin, part of me remained the good little girl trying to earn other people's approval. That little girl in me didn't want to stop trying to measure up to all those voices in my head. As an adult, I had never fully given myself permission to be the person I had always felt myself to be, never showed up for myself the way I had tried to show up to other people's ideas of what my life should look like. I thought I was choosing Love, but actually fear had chosen my life for me, and I had spent fifty years grooving its long and rutted road to inner misery.

Changing that wasn't going to be easy. But at least now I understood what I had to do. The time had finally come, to riff on my dad's favorite expression, to shit or get off the proverbial ancient black Etruscan pot!

What Happens Next

So I did—in the most unlikely of ways.

Five years to the day after my wake-up call in the mirror, my landlord contacted me out of the blue letting me know that he had to sell the house where I had been living. A few years earlier, I had rented a wonderful modern light-filled townhouse surrounded by shimmering aspen trees with a lovely view of the mountains. I loved it there so much that I hoped to buy it as soon as I had saved enough money. No matter how many nights I spent on the road, my Santa Fe home remained my sanctuary. I was terrified to lose that sweet space that felt like my safe haven.

This time, however, I knew that a wake-up call means one thing and one thing only: You have to wake up!

Two months later, I embarked on a life of intentional homelessness.

When I tell people that I am intentionally homeless, they rarely know how to process it. They listen, they nod, and then they always ask, "But where do you live?"

"No," I reply, "I mean it. I am literally intentionally homeless. As in I sold almost everything I own, and I live on the road. I couch surf, I take jobs that come with lodging included—I just figure it out one day at a time. I'm living life without a safety net. I don't have a steady job, so some months I don't even know how my bills will get paid. Depending on where I am and what I'm doing, I either feel like I'm having the greatest adventure in the world, or like I'm completely nuts."

"Wow!" they say. "Just wow!"

Then folks have one of three responses: "I am so jealous. I would love to do that!" "That sounds incredible, but I could never do that!" or the most frequent response: a blank stare of complete incomprehension followed by a palpable wave of discomfort before changing the subject.

I don't blame them. When I walked away from my home in the spring of 2016, I imagined my adventurous new life on the road as an epic Technicolor Cinemascope extravaganza. In reality, it's been more like the Coen Brothers meet the Wachowskis— and even that feels a little too glamorous. Truth is, real life never looks like the movies. There's no cameraman capturing the desultory me trudging down a fluorescent-lit supermarket aisle in a strange town fighting the urge to buy a family-sized bag of chips because I have the ridiculous idea that those chips will make me feel better about the loneliness I often feel living on the road. No one is going to film an Academy Award–winning short about the disheartened me who, at 4:30 every afternoon, doesn't know what to do with the impending darkness, not of night, but of doubt. There's not even call for a life-affirming docudrama about the hopeful early-morning me curled up with her faithful dog at her side while journaling her morning spiritual practice, as she has done for the past two decades. Even my intentional homelessness isn't grungy and depressing enough for an arty indie film shot in grainy black and white.

We waste huge portions of our lives acting out narratives that try to replicate all those larger-than-life stories we see on the screen. Sooner or later, however, we learn that it is impossible to live those fictions and feel anything but miserable. We wonder why our lives don't look like cinematic spectacles filled with poster-perfect people and preposterous plots. When our everyday lives don't match those unlivable models, we can't help but ask ourselves: Is that why I am so unhappy?

This is the reason most of us have a hard time knowing how to change our lives: We have no road maps, no models for what happens after our wake-up calls. No one makes movies about what happens next because what happens next is almost always decidedly unglamorous. No one wants to watch that film!

We want to see life's highs, to assure us they exist. We empathize with the lows, because they make us feel less alone. Escape? You bet! Bring on the studly superheroes and even the twisted monsters, the epic journeys and the fantastic voyages.

What no one tells us is that it is, in fact, our seemingly unremarkable daily existences that we are here to live—to which we *have* to show up if we ever hope to look ourselves in the eye and feel that we are living our best lives. Only by showing up to our own lives as our truest selves can we contribute to the well-being of the world. It is that simple and that complex: To save the planet, we must save ourselves first.

The perpetual quandary for us all is how to live the changes we wish to make. No one else's path is ours, and no one else can walk it for us. We can be inspired, get maps, gather ideas, ask advice, be companioned along the way, but then we have to risk doing it. You. Me. We have to risk doing it. No one else can do it for us. That can feel lonely, scary, and wildly uncomfortable—at best!

⁓

Since that moment in the mirror seven years ago when I decided it was time for a major change, my life has played out as a perpetual (and certainly not always pretty) tug of war between my false and true selves. Still, I wouldn't change a minute: the falling apart, the rebuilding, the try-and-try-againing, even when I felt as though I rarely succeeded. I wouldn't change anything I went through because every step has led me exactly to where I have needed to go—right here, right now, right wherever I am. That's been the hardest lesson for me to learn.

On the road trip of my life, my desired destination had always been anywhere but my own heart. To finally live my best life as my truest self, I had to learn to love whatever surfaced, instead of continually creating myself in the image and likeness of other people.

Mostly, I had to stop believing what my mother seemed to believe—that perfect was actually possible. Though my heart always knew better, my mind had internalized her perfectionism so completely that some part of me actually thought that surely there must be One Right Way, which, if I could only find it, would make everything better.

It took me years to understand that my mother hated all the things that were broken in herself, which was why she was so terrified of my untidy enthusiasms, my outside-the-box interests, my risky adventurings, my inability to shut up. I had to learn to forgive and release my mother's teachings—prompted by love yet forged in fear—and instead trust the inner wisdom that transcends all of our human histories.

Instead of paving over my inner paradise and taking up residence in someone else's parking lot, I had to follow my heart out onto the open highway. There, on this road trip back to my truest self, I have lost my way, my faith, my religion, my reputation, my bearings, my cool, my shirt, my shit, my grip, my thread, my mind, my marbles, my nerve, my temper, my lunch, and my footing. I have lost touch, lost time, lost ground, lost count, lost track, lost favor, lost heart, lost patience, lost out, lost contact. This wild and crazy ride is what I have come to call the Way of Being Lost.

Where the Rubber Meets the Road

Turns out, to live as our truest selves, we have to be willing to become lost.

On some level, that seems completely paradoxical. To find ourselves, we have to lose ourselves?

Well, yes. To know the truth that sets us free means that we must learn to embrace all the pain and struggle along the way, trusting that it, too—perhaps even it above all—will get us where we long to be. Paradox always paves the path back to our truest selves.

It took me a while, but I finally got it in such a way that I never doubted it again: *To find your way home to your authentic true self and live your best life, you have to be willing to get lost to all of the myriad small, false, misguided selves the world has told you to spend your whole life becoming.*

So if we want to be found but we must begin by getting lost, then how do we get lost? As we all know, getting lost just happens. One moment you're sure you're five minutes from your desired destination, and then next thing you know, you're in the middle of nowhere with no clue how you got there or what to do to get home.

That's the bummer and the beauty of it all: There is no road map for the Way of Being Lost.

You can't get lost on purpose, but you must get purposefully lost.

We can't haul ourselves out to the nearest forest in a blinding snowstorm without jackets, maps, or water and then wander around telling the Universe we're ready to be lost in order to be found—while in actuality we're really just in a full-blown panic imagining we're going to die of hypothermia and no one will ever find us.

The Way of Being Lost is a conscious, considered, co-creative, collaborative act. The first step is to acknowledge to ourselves, to anyone else we trust to hear us from their hearts, and to whatever Higher Power we believe in that we have lost someone essential and precious—our true self. Then the next thing we must do is make a commitment to find her.

No matter what.

Most of the time, however, we actively try anything we can to avoid this life-changing path home to our true selves. We have to die to our small false learned selves to let our true selves live? We have to get lost over and over again in order to be found? Who's going to sign up for that? Surely, we all think—I certainly did—there has to be a better way!

There isn't.

Although the Way of Being Lost may feel like the last resort, in truth it's the only resort. None of us wants to believe that—until one day we find ourselves at the same old, same old, dead-end place from which we have turned back and run like hell so many times before. Only then will we know that we have reached the point of no return where all the guidebooks are no longer of use because we are in such uncharted territory.

Slowly it sinks in. We have to throw away all the old road maps and trust our truest selves to lead us back home.

So how do we get to this place of being lost enough to start becoming found?

Well, that's why it's called the Way of Being Lost. You can't plan it. It just happens—usually when you least expect it. When it does, you realize that there really is only one way to go: forward into the seemingly complete unknown where we finally, and seemingly miraculously, discover the courage to hear what we have been too terrified to admit: I am lost.

From there—from that place that none of us ever aspires to be, but which we will come to discover is the hopeful and healing embarkation point for all fundamental transformation—the rubber finally meets the road.

At last, we find ourselves on the beautiful but bumpy, healing but hard, radical but redemptive Way of Being Lost.

PART ONE

REMEMBERING JOY

We need Joy as we need air.
We need Love as we need water.
We need each other as we need the earth we share.

—Maya Angelou

1

WRITING
MYSELF WHOLE

Ever since I was a little girl, I have wanted to write the kind of books that could sing to other people's hearts in the ways that books have sung to mine. Growing up, I read books voraciously. I loved to get lost in the people, the places, and the stories I discovered on every printed page.

My favorite Christmas or birthday present was always the same: a $10 gift certificate from my dad to Hunter's Books—my childhood Mecca on the corner of Little Santa Monica and Rodeo Drive in Beverly Hills, in what is now some of the highest-priced commercial real estate in the world. Twice a year, my dad took me to this treasure trove filled with printed little worlds, inviting me to come away with whatever precious written jewels called to me. He let me take as long as I wanted—understanding that each choice was an investment in my soul. When I emerged with ten whole books that were all mine, I was gleaming with joy. I couldn't wait to get home and disappear into all of the worlds that I was carrying—whole worlds that fit into the arms of a mere child.

In the days following our excursion, I barely left my room. I dove in and didn't surface until I was completely sated. Then I couldn't wait to tell my dad about everything I had discovered. But first, each and every time, we had the same sweet exchange.

"Dad!" I would exclaim, having run down to find him in his sunny study. "I've finished them all!"

"What?" he would reply in pretend shock. "All of them? All ten of them?"

"Yes! All ten of them!"

"I spent ten whole dollars, and you've used that all up in three days?" he would playfully continue. "I sure don't feel like I got a lot of bang for my buck if you finished all those books in three days! That gift was supposed to last you for months."

His smile always belied his words. I knew he was proud that I loved books and words and ideas and stories as much as he did. That I consumed them with an appetite for life that matched his own omnivorous curiosity for everything. I would smile in sheepish glee at being his bookish spendthrift, and then we would settle in to one of our wonderful conversations about my literary adventures.

With every childhood book I read, I fell more and more in love with the power of words. To be a writer seemed to me the most amazing profession in the world. Writers could be everyone kids want to be all rolled up in one—a medieval knight in armor, a Native American girl stranded on a rocky island, a talking spider who befriends a pig. I dreamed of one day writing my own books that would allow other people to feel the pure wonder, immense awe, and hopeful anticipation I always experienced when I got lost in a story.

As I grew older, I began to write my own poems and plays, short stories and essays. I wrote to make sense of the world, to bring to consciousness all that I hoped and feared, dreaded and desired. I wrote to understand what I wanted to know, what I believed to be true, what I dared to imagine. When I thought about what I hoped to do with my life, I could think of nothing truer, more loving, and more hopeful than to put words on a page that might inspire someone to live more fully and love more deeply, that could cradle a person through their fears and hold their hand in hope and healing.

In my late twenties, I found a job that gave me both the financial resources and the free time to write—a ridiculous job cold-calling people on the phone and selling them things they didn't need. A job in which I earned more money than I have ever earned in my whole life—even now. A job that ended at 1 PM, allowing me to rent a writing studio where I spent every afternoon doing what I had always wanted to do. But every time I sat down to write, all I felt was pressure. The easy joy I had always found in words vanished every time I faced a blank page. My friends were writing award-winning books, movies, and television shows. I, however, suddenly had no earthly idea what I even *wanted* to write. I felt completely stuck.

When you love something as much as I loved books, what you love and the people who do what you love can assume an almost magical power. If writers were wizards who could conjure up worlds from words, instead of letting their magic inspire my own, I convinced myself that I would never be able to live up to the exaltation in which I held their high art.

Then, in my mid-30s, I finally wrote a book. On and off during my twenties, my dad and I had worked together on a collection of essays about the visual arts—a topic that had become our shared passion. After his death in 1993, however, the publishers asked me to write his biography instead. I don't think children can ever be truly objective enough to be their parents' biographers. I certainly wasn't. But because I couldn't bear the thought of not sharing his wonderful stories and cultural contributions with the world, I agreed.

When the book turned out to be a success, I started writing celebrity biographies for television and signed two contracts to write books about other famous Hollywood actors. Having dreamed of becoming a working writer, I should have felt ecstatic. Instead, just a couple of years later I called my agent to report that I was despondent. "I *hate* what I am writing," I told her. "I don't ever go in the biography section of the bookstore. I don't even watch television. I have no idea why I'm doing this."

To her immense credit, she heard me. "Good. I'm glad you know that," she told me. "Now go off and figure out what you do want to write. I can't wait to read it." Neither she nor I thought it would take me another fifteen years. Paradoxically, her permission paralyzed me from the wrist down. Instead of feeling free to be me, I stumbled headlong into a two-decade case of chronic writer's block.

When I was a little girl who felt lonely because her parents were always away, who felt peculiar because she wasn't like the other kids, who felt nerdy because she loved learning more than being cool, who felt isolated because she lived behind big walls

6

with no next-door neighbors to play with, who felt overprotected because her parents feared the perils of their own fame, books were my closest friends.

No matter how I came to a book—in loneliness or confusion, in isolation or fear—I left in love. Books healed whatever ailed me and inspired me to live the life of my dreams.

They still do.

This is not a book *about* my spiritual journey. This book *is* my spiritual journey. This book is the literal literary manifestation of the lifelong pilgrimage on which I have lost my religion but found my spirit; lost my mind but found my heart; lost my words but found my way; lost my grip but found my freedom; lost my shit but found my shine.

Healing happens when we understand that what we are seeking has been inside us all along—waiting for us to live and love it back whole. In order to write a book that heals, I had to heal my own life by writing this book.

When I embarked upon a road trip to rediscover the voice of my truest self, I had to learn to hear her stories and then find the courage to speak them out into the world. Only by speaking true could I begin to lose the life-limiting narratives that had hogtied me to my false self and paralyzed my creativity. Only by writing myself whole have I begun to *live* myself whole.

"Nothing in the world has as much power as a word," Emily Dickinson once said. "Sometimes I write one, and I look at it until it begins to shine." By finally writing this book in my truest words of my truest self, my life has begun to shine.

That's not to say that writing this book hasn't felt scary. To speak truth is always scary. To speak truth when a lot of voices in your head are telling you to shut up feels flat-out terrifying. But way, way more frightening would be not to have written this book at all.

I have spent a lifetime finding inspiration in words whose magic has shone off the page and into my soul. At the end of the day, however, the healing I had always been seeking all came down to one word.

One magic word.

A word whose power and presence and possibility I had all but forgotten—until the summer of 2011.

To keep the promise I made to myself in the mirror and finally show up to my own life, I had to rediscover my magic word.

2

MAGIC
WORDS

My introduction to the idea of magic words came early.
We were sitting in my mom's car, parked under a tall thin palm tree outside a pale-cream stucco house on Foothill Road in Beverly Hills. Five-year-old me was squirming with excitement in my favorite smocked yellow party dress and white patent leather shoes, my long blonde hair pulled back tightly with a matching yellow bow. I couldn't wait to go inside!

I loved birthday parties because they provided one of the few occasions where I could be with my school friends outside of the classroom—to play games, giggle about silly things, and eat the big globs of brightly colored frosting no one else wanted off of everyone's pieces of cake.

My parents and I lived in a 9,000-square-foot Spanish mansion inside a gated compound on a quarter acre in nearby Beverly Glen canyon. There were no sidewalks. We didn't know our next-door neighbors. I couldn't ride my bike around the block to meet my friends or down to the store to buy candy. I only got to be with kids my age at school or other extracurricular activities like ballet or cotillion or horseback riding. That's why birthday parties were so special. With no lessons to be learned, we were just there to have fun—together.

Other cars were pulling up all around us. I watched my classmates run up the path, clutching their presents, and ring the front bell. I saw the door open and Mrs. Moss usher each one in. But my mother had something to ask before she would let me out of the car: "What are you going to remember to say while you are there?"

That was easy.

"'Please' and 'thank you.'" I knew those magic words. I reached for the door handle.

My mother wasn't finished.

"And what are you going to do when the party is over?" she queried.

In 1960s Southern California, my salt-and-pepper-haired British mother—born in 1917 in the Edwardian Age to Victorian parents—was a throwback to another era. She sent me to a school where we curtseyed to the principal every morning underneath the American flag. She painstakingly taught me which fork and knife went with what course at fancy dinner parties, and then she watched in despair as I hunched over dinner in front of the TV and shoveled food in my mouth while trading bites with my dad. She was determined that my manners be impeccable with every adult I met. So I knew the answer. But I was way more focused on the party than on my mother's life lessons.

"I am going to find Mrs. Moss and thank her," I replied distractedly.

My mother didn't say anything. She just looked at me, unflinching, waiting for the right answer this time.

I just wanted to go inside and be with my friends. But I turned around and faced her, trying to tame my impatience. I knew I had to reassure her that I knew the lines of my script—the other magic words of childhood politesse that would allow my mom to let me go to the party.

"I will go find Mrs. Moss and say, 'Thank you for letting me come,'" I said, in what I hoped seemed a genuinely contrite tone of voice.

My mother smiled. "That's right," she responded, reassured at last. "Never forget to say those words to the hostess of any party you attend."

I was already halfway out of the car.

⌒

I don't remember anything else about that birthday party other than the ending. As the other kids were getting ready to leave, I began searching for Mrs. Moss. I walked over and earnestly looked up at her.

"Mrs. Moss," I politely began.

Mrs. Moss looked down at me expectantly, as though waiting for a request—perhaps another glass of bright red punch or maybe the location of the restroom. She was, like most of the other mothers in our class, at least twenty years younger than my mom. She had big frosted hair and wore a short, brightly colored dress like the ones I saw on television. She was beautiful.

"Thank you for letting me come."

Her whole face broke into a big smile.

"Why thank you, Victoria. Aren't you sweet?" she responded, as though truly touched by my remark. "Please come back any time. We would love to have you."

I beamed back at her, genuinely surprised and pleased by her enthusiastic reaction. The only reason I had gone over to her was that I knew the first thing my mother would ask me was whether I had followed her script. Seeing Mrs. Moss smile, I suddenly wondered if there wasn't something to what my mother had been going on about all along. Those six words strung together had made this beautiful woman stop and see me in ways that made me stand out from the other kids. They had a magical effect. It was the first time that I understood that certain words could elicit special responses.

From then on, at every party, I always went over and ingratiated myself with every mother by uttering that same polite sentence: *Thank you for letting me come.* Without fail, their response always seemed to elicit the same genuine delight.

Fifty years later, as I career through life trying to tick things off my daily to-do list, I still always say "please" and express my gratitude in whatever version of "Thank you for letting me come" seems appropriate. "Please" still always stops people in their tracks. "Thank you" still always elicits genuine delight because gratitude breaks down all walls and connects me with whomever I am speaking. Turns out, as she was in so many ways that irritated the rebellious younger me, my mother was right. There really *are* magic words.

It's just that now I understand how the magic works. These are heart-based words. They acknowledge something our heart desires or that our heart has received; they show appreciation for the actions of others. They reflect our hearts out to other hearts. As such, they act as a pause button on the inner monologues usually going through our busy, worried, frantic, anxious, doubtful heads—and return us, however briefly, to the one place every single one of us secretly longs to live: in Love.

When we were little, it sure seemed easier to live heart-based lives. But as we grow up, so much of what we learn in school, in books, and on television begins to lure us into our heads. One particular word seems to be the biggest culprit—the word *should*.

The older we get, the more we start thinking about how we should act, what we should be feeling, what we should wear, how we should look, what classes we should take, what college we should attend, what job we should want, what kind of relationship we should have. By taking us out of our hearts, and into our worried and anxious heads, shoulding does its level best to erode Love.

Here's the good news. It can't. No matter how dedicated we are to our should lists, Love always wins. If (and this is the kicker) we do whatever it takes to keep our hearts open, whether it's by doing something as simple as saying "please" and "thank you" or by discovering our own special magic word.

3
MY MAGIC
WORD

Half a lifetime later, however, standing in front of that mirror in my slate-grey bathroom, my heart felt so closed that I had no idea how or if it would ever reopen. But my promise to show up to my own life was more than just a promise. It was also a prayer. I knew I needed help.

I got it.

I got it big time.

It came in the unlikeliest of ways—in the form of *my* magic word.

After my wake-up call in the mirror, I had no idea what to do next. Fortunately, my true self did. If we get quiet and listen, we can hear our truest selves saying, "Turn left," "This doesn't feel right," "That's not you at all. This is," or "Go for it!" Truth is broadcasting 24/7, but most of the time we're too busy listening to the static of our busy lives to tune in.

When we do . . . well, all I can say is *wow!*

Two months after my conversation with myself in the mirror, I stood up in front of a wildly enthusiastic standing-room-only audience at the Missouri History Museum in St. Louis on what would have been Vincent Price's 100th birthday. There in his beloved hometown, I spoke for two hours about the loving, generous, joyful, fun, clever, interested, interesting, funny, curious, wonderful person I knew as Dad. I then spent the rest of 2011 traveling the world to continue this celebration at a series of events dubbed the Vincentennial (the name still brings a smile to my face).

Twelve years earlier, I had gone out on two long U.S. and U.K. book tours in support of my biography about my dad, sharing stories of my father's life and career with his fans. This time the thought came, *Do something different—something that makes your heart sing.* Instead of talking about what my father had done in his career, I decided to talk about how he had lived his life.

Although there certainly were movie stars more famous, more talented, and more successful than Vincent Price had been during his 65-year career, what had made him so special then— and still so beloved now—was the way he moved through the world. That's what I wanted to share.

Vincent Price had one of the longest careers in Hollywood. Although he was known for his many contributions to film, radio, television, and the visual and culinary arts, I believe the most extraordinary thing about my dad was how joyfully and generously he lived his life.

My dad's joy was infectious. He made you believe that life was an incredible adventure and all any of us had to do to enjoy it was to dive in wholeheartedly. He found his greatest joy in encouraging and inspiring people to live their truest lives—whatever they might be. He made people believe in the power of good—which is pretty ironic for one of the most famous bad guys in movie history. I truly believe if each of us could spend even five minutes living with half as much generosity and kindness as my father, the world would be a better place.

To those who did not know my dad or who are not Vincent Price fans, perhaps that sounds like hyperbolic hero worship. I've now spent five decades talking with thousands of people who knew and were inspired by my father, and they all say the same thing: Vincent Price was one of the kindest, most generous, joy-filled, life-affirming people they have ever known. In an industry where backstabbing and gossip and judgment are the norm, that's pretty amazing. Those same qualities came through in every movie, radio show, interview, and television appearance; in all of the lectures he gave; as well as in the syndicated newspaper column and many books he wrote. They earned him a large and loyal fandom and were the reason his 100th birthday was being celebrated all around the world almost twenty years after his death.

On that night in St. Louis after I spoke, people stood in line for two hours to share their own inspirational Vincent Price stories with me. It was one of the most magical evenings of my life. I *felt* his presence—not like he was in the room, but like he was in *me*. What I felt that evening was pure joy!

That joy continued all year long. For the rest of 2011, I traveled to places I had longed to visit—like Ireland and Wales. I met and shared adventures with incredible people and talked with them about my dad and how he lived his life. I had the kinds of deep, joy-filled, honest conversations I had been craving for so long about creativity and inspiration and curiosity. The formerly miserable 48-year-old me who had spent every waking hour working to pay back debt and stave off guilt and shame began to transform into a hopeful, joyful, connected, enthusiastic, interested 49-year-old, who was learning, once again, how to communicate with, as, through, and in her truest self. It was one of the best years of my life, because I remembered my native tongue, my heart language, my magic word: I remembered my joy.

I have come to believe that each of us enters this world encoded with our own intuitive "language" through which we speak, see, understand, and interpret everything and everyone around us—through which we share our hearts with one another and with our whole planet.

This native tongue is actually a language beyond words that we never need to be taught. It is the language of our true selves, with which we engage in all the conversations we were meant to have, through which we make the connections that feed our souls and help us work the work, play the play, and live the lives we know we are meant to be living.

Then we grow up.

We start speaking the world's languages—the ones that keep us working the world's work, playing the world's games, living the world's lives. These are the languages of commerce and competition and conquest. We start forgetting we ever had a native tongue.

So when we rediscover it, we need to pay attention and promise to keep listening. Only by remembering our native tongues can we begin living our best lives as our truest selves.

4

CHOOSING
JOY

That summer of the Vincentennial, I was on a flight from Santa Fe to Los Angeles. It was a small plane, the kind that feels like a paper towel tube crammed with oversized people packed cheek-to-jowl, hurtling through the air 38,000 feet above the earth. On our descent, our plane suddenly made an alarmingly steep dip and then began to climb erratically. You always wonder what you will do if your plane does something totally scary. As we careened through the ether on our improbably bucking bronco, no one made a sound. We all grabbed our armrests and held on for what we prayed was dear life—not daring to acknowledge, by looking into one another's eyes, what we all feared: *Was this it?*

Interestingly, I felt totally calm—until the plane leveled out. Then, when the pilots didn't bother to tell us what the hell had just happened, the panic rose up in my throat. We all began to talk to one another to reassure ourselves that we were going to be OK. That's when the guy next to me said, "Don't worry! I fly all the time, so I went to a psychic who assured me that I'm not going to die in a plane crash." Well, that sounded like as good an excuse as any to breathe a massive sigh of relief and let go of the fear. The two of us settled into a conversation.

He was on his way to Australia to be a speaker at a huge conference on the same platform as the Dalai Lama. *Wow!* I thought. *How cool is that?!* I asked him more about what he did. As he described writing the kinds of books that inspired people to live their best lives and then going around the world speaking about that, I recognized: *That's what I have always wanted to do!*

In that moment, I set my intention to find a way to share the life-changing joy I was experiencing through the Vincentennial with a larger audience. This was how I would finally begin showing up to my own life and contributing something meaningful to the world.

When 2011 came to an end, however, that didn't feel as easy as it had seemed while I was on the road following in my father's footsteps. My father expressed joy in an almost effortless way, and accessing my own joy in memory of his seemed just as effortless. Things didn't feel quite the same when I got home. As it all turns out, misery really does love company—and the company that our misery loves the most is our own.

Misery needs us to stay up into the wee hours of the morning with her and hash through all the reasons why she is our best friend. After the Vincentennial, without my father's shoes to fill, suddenly the ways in which he lived his life began to fade from my consciousness, only to be quickly replaced by anxiety, stress, overwork, debt, and discontent. That old miserable me I thought I had left behind resurfaced, drowning out my nascent joy with her old familiar fears.

Who do you think you are?
What makes you think you can live the life of your dreams?
Are you willing to risk losing everything all over again just to follow your heart?

⌒

Two years later, I found myself on another paper-towel-tube plane—this time from Santa Fe to Dallas. I was heading to Atlanta to give a talk on design. I thought that the man sitting across from me looked familiar. Suddenly I realized he had been the guy on that L.A. flight who had given me my epiphany.

We settled into another conversation. I told him that he had helped me discover what I wanted to do when I grew up. This time I asked him how he had created the life he was now living. He shared that he had found a formula that worked: writing about famous people in history in such a way that inspired people through the lessons learned from their lives. He made it sound so simple. He had found what he loved doing, and then he'd just shown up and done it.

I, on the other hand, still recovering from my financial meltdown eight years earlier, was juggling three businesses—creating my public speaking career, running a retail art gallery and design studio, and doing interior design/construction project management for clients around the country.

I never took a day off. I averaged four hours of sleep a night and worked eighteen hour days. I felt like I could never catch up, even though I was running as fast as I could. My whole life had become one unending cycle of work, work, work. I had forgotten how to do anything else. I was exhausted. I had become a workaholic.

21

In the wake of all my financial losses a decade earlier, I had begun working as hard and as long and as much as I could in my determination to rebuild my life. My dedication paid off. Not only did I begin reducing my debt, but I also succeeded in numbing much of the guilt and shame I felt. I genuinely believed that the more work I took on, the better I would feel. It wasn't until I lost one of my dearest friends to addiction that I realized what was really happening.

I had been mainlining work as a means of assuaging my anxiety—not only about my finances, but also about all of the uncertainty in my life. I wasn't seeing that what alcohol or drugs does for other people, work did for me. It pulled focus from my fear and gave me the artificial sense of security found in doing doing doing. But ultimately, the anxiety remained. Underneath my colossal workload and industrial-strength work ethic, I was becoming more and more stressed, more and more miserable. I felt like I was on the verge of breaking apart into a million pieces that I couldn't ever put back together again.

Something had to give. I knew what it was.

I needed to reconnect with the joy I had felt during the Vincentennial.

5

THE PURE AND SIMPLE DELIGHT IN BEING ALIVE

Words are like colors. We can all agree that green is the color of leaves or grass, or golf courses or dollar bills for that matter. But what I picture when I say green may be very different from what, say, a golfer or a Wall Street banker might have in their mind's eye. It's the same with joy. Each of us experiences and expresses it uniquely.

I knew what joy felt like when I was following in my father's footsteps. When I talked with his fans and traveled the world giving inspirational talks, I felt the joy of adventure, new encounters, and meaningful connections. I also found joy in my work with my interior design clients—getting to know them deeply so that I could co-create their living and working spaces to reflect their truest selves. What I didn't know how to do was find joy when I wasn't working or traveling or doing things for other people. So I began where I always begin anything—with words. I read everything I could get my hands on by anyone who had ever written anything about joy.

Although innumerable definitions of joy exist, I found the one I loved the best: Joy is the pure and simple delight in being alive. That captures exactly how joy feels to me: the *Wheeeeeeee!!* and the wisdom, the curiosity and the quiet, the ecstasy and the ease. Even the word "delight" makes me feel, well, like jumping for joy! That's because joy is a *felt* thing. Joy may be sparked by, brought to life through, and flourish in our experiences—but ultimately joy exists within each of us apart from whatever has happened to evoke it. We are all born fluent in joy. When we feel joy, we feel in sync with the Universe— which means, of course, that the Universe is in sync with us. Joy blesses us all.

I have always felt that joy and happiness were quite different emotions. Fraternal twins. Happiness, it has always seemed to me, is dependent on something outside of us. It's transient and somewhat self-involved. Even if we share our happiness with other people, we often experience it inside ourselves in a way that can make us want to hoard and protect it. We hang on to happiness as though it were our favorite amusement park balloon that could pull loose at any second and float into the ether, leaving us on the ground caterwauling for its loss.

Joy, on the other hand, is what many have called a "soul feeling." It comes from the inside out—that flowering tendril growing out from our hearts and wrapping itself in brightly colored delight around and up everything it meets. To feel joy is to experience our own well-being as linked to that of the larger world, to sense that we move through life as something other than our egos. Joy is the great connector.

Each of us is born with the light of joy—a light that we may sometimes fear has been buried in the accumulated darkness of our doubts and disappointments. When we can pause long enough to silence our tendency to fret, worry, and complain—and instead be grateful for what we do have, rather than focused on what we don't—we always remember our joy. Even on my crappiest days, if I can remind myself to feel the bedrock of good that underlies my life, this planet, and the people and other creatures with whom I share it, what I feel beneath that day's supposed woes is the good, the joy, the gratitude, the balance, the hope, the peace, and the love that have never gone anywhere.

Mark Twain believed that "to get the full value of joy, you must have someone to divide it with." You can never completely experience joy unless you share it with others and they share it with you. Joy is the ultimate renewable resource. To hoard joy is impossible, because only when we share it will it flourish and grow. To get the full value of any life-affirming experience, we have to give part of it away as well as receive it from someone or something else.

Too often, however, the innate joy with which we come into the world gets plastered and painted over by our concerned parents, our well-meaning teachers, our peer-pressuring friends. Then one day we start to forget what's underneath all that plaster and paint. We even start to think that plastering and painting is what we came here to do. It's not. When we cease and desist our human doings and instead inhabit our human being, we remember our joy.

In this materialistic age of technological advances and disposable everything, however, we can fall into the trap of believing that joy can be found in things. But that new car I just *had* to have or even the latest iPhone I believed would change my life—a few years from now they will be long gone. Worse still, the exorbitant monthly payments for these "necessities" have, more often than not, robbed me of the joy I hoped they would bring. When I remember that the reason I coveted the car in the first place was to be able to go to the places that bring me joy with the people with whom I wish to share it, and that the conversations or photos or music for which my iPhone was the conduit were what brought me joy, then the choices I make begin to shift. I remember that it's not the thing that I want at all, but rather the joy. That joy is already in me.

Leave it to Mother Teresa to get to the heart of joy by describing the joy of the heart: "A joyful heart is the normal result of a heart bursting with love. She gives most who gives with joy." Joy and love are the double helix of our lives. One cannot exist without the other. To feel joy is to feel love. To feel love is to feel joy. To be of service, to reach out to a friend, to offer a hug, to hold the hand of someone in sorrow is to bring joy to sorrow and love to fear. Joy is being at the bedside of someone in pain or listening to their woes with a compassionate heart. The more joy we feel, the more we are able to give. In the giving, our joy is replenished—because its supply is inexhaustible.

At the end of the day, joy is what connects you to me and me to you right now. On this very page that I am writing and you are reading, joy leaps the time-space continuum just as it transcends national boundaries and political divisions. It knows no age or religion, skin color or calorie count. Joy is our home and our vacation, our vocation and our hobby. Joy is the channel through which Love flows just as Love is the channel through which joy flows. Which is to say, joy is everything.

Joy is a common language spoken heart-to-heart by all sentient beings, who feel the pure and simple delight in being alive that keeps us all connected to everyone and everything and to the Universe as a whole.

The more I read and thought about joy, the more I *felt* joy. Joy felt amazing, elating, hopeful, connected, freeing—everything I had hoped to feel when I vowed to change my life. Joy felt like the conduit from my head to my heart to the heart of the whole wide world.

I began talking about joy to anyone who would listen. I talked about finding more joy in my life. I talked about writing about joy. I talked about talking about joy more in my talks. I talked about the importance of joy as our heart connection to the planet. I talked and I talked and I talked *a lot* about joy.

But talking about joy is not living joy.

The fact is, I talked about joy because it felt a lot easier to talk about joy than to really live it.

Then one day it didn't.

After four years of trying and failing, of working and working and working while thinking about but never fully experiencing my joy, I finally had had enough!

At the end of 2014—almost four years since my conversation with myself in the mirror impelled me to change my life—I decided that come hell or high water or both, I was going to show up to joy every single damn day. I had no idea what that meant. I just couldn't stand hearing the sound of my own hopeful promises reverberating against the increasingly joyless walls of my life any longer. It was time to say goodbye to fear-based workaholism and invite joy back in for good.

6

THE WINGED
WARRIOR
OF DELIGHT

"I'm going to make joy my life focus," I announced enthusiastically to my closest friends. "I'm going to practice joy, preach joy, live joy. It's all about joy for me now. Joy to the world—literally. It's going to be 24/7 joy!"

Their response was surprisingly underwhelming.

A few politely nodded and vaguely smiled. One or two cocked their heads in confusion like my dog does when she hears a high-pitched noise. Others were just flat-out resistant.

"Joy feels like too much pressure," one friend said.

"I actually hate the word 'joy'," said another. "It's too, well, joyful."

"The word 'joy' makes me feel I'm a failure at my own life," shared a third.

As quickly as my joy enthusiasm had waxed, just as quickly it waned: "I guess I'll just find time for joy later," I heard myself say with alarming regularity as I submerged myself in more and more work. That's when the Universe intervened in the form of a big brick wall that knocked me flat.

Toward the end of a five-week speaking and appearance tour in the fall of 2014, I got a cold. I soldiered on, yet I felt worse and worse. But a cold wasn't going to stop me. I had appearances and meetings with clients. I made it through them all, and with the selfless help of my friend Cynthia, who drove my car and me back to Santa Fe, I finally made it home. Then I just collapsed.

Over the course of the next few weeks, as I began to recuperate, I felt filled with fear. Not as much about what was happening in my body as about how bad my workaholism had gotten once again. I had made all these changes in order to do all the kinds of things I was now doing—travel and touring and talks—but I was still working my miserable self to the bone.

The message came through loud and clear: *You cannot keep doing this to yourself!*

As November turned into December, I regained strength. I began to feel grateful for what had happened. Being that ill had given me a reset button, a chance to do things differently. I could stop muscling my way through life and instead begin trusting my true self to guide me toward healthier, more life-affirming choices. I vowed that things would be different in the new year.

January didn't even end before I was back at my old habit. Working, working, working. Traveling, traveling, traveling. Pushing myself as hard as I could push.

⁓

Fortunately, when the Universe decides to get your attention, She always succeeds. During the middle of an otherwise routine phone conversation, my then-business partner Dawn happened to mention that she wanted to take a course with a woman in Santa Fe who taught motivational speaking. Everyone who was anyone in the inspirational speaking world had taken it, Dawn told me.

When she mentioned the teacher's name—Gail Larsen—I was incredulous. I played tennis with someone who had the same name! For the life of me, I couldn't imagine my Gail as a world-famous inspirational speaking teacher. I went on her website to check it out. Nope. Not the same person.

That's when I read these questions on her website:

Are you ready to...

✤ Stretch to the size of your calling?
✤ Find your way to speak powerfully about what you love?
✤ Let your communications reflect who you really are?
✤ Permit your authentic self to emerge in front of your audience?
✤ Trust yourself to speak well in the moment?

I needed to take this course myself! I wanted to speak what I loved, live my calling, and be more of my authentic self—and what I loved and wanted to speak powerfully about was joy. I just wasn't doing it. I was working far too hard at everything except what mattered the most to my heart.

So I did what I often do when I have a big and exciting idea. I called my then-82-year-old joy co-conspirator and soul friend Mary. When I decided to change my life, Mary had been my biggest cheerleader, not only rooting me on from the sidelines, but also often being instrumental in co-creating opportunities for many of my greatest experiences. She seemed to be the one person who really got it when I talked about joy.

"Go for it!" she told me.

So I did. Over Valentine's Day weekend 2015, I spent four intensive days with five other women learning not only how to communicate our passion to others in transformational ways, but perhaps even more importantly, how to communicate our passion to ourselves so that we could hear it, trust it, and then speak it.

Right from the get-go, I fell in love with my classmates—their stories, their energy, and their willingness to get down and dirty in the muck and mire of transformation. It was so easy to tell all of them about my joy mission that I forgot all about the naysayers inside and outside of my head. In that safe and supportive environment, everyone's enthusiasm about my joy message lit me up in hope!

<hr />

One of the first things Gail does in the workshop is help people name and claim what she calls their Original Medicine. Only from that knowing can she guide her students into the place from which each of them can speak truth through their hearts.

When I heard her term "Original Medicine," I felt a tad cynical. Was this going to be one of those touchy-feely things with smudging, drumming, and dream catchers where I would end up with some ridiculous name like She Who Skips Joyfully with Aardvarks? I told myself to keep an open mind about what seemed like some pretty woo-woo cultural appropriation, but I was prepared to have a wry chuckle at the whole process and then get on with learning what I thought I was there to learn. Hah!

As my heart cracked open that weekend, everything I heard and learned went straight in—including my Original Medicine. On the first day, we paired up with a classmate. I got Carly, a thirty-something student of *A Course in Miracles* with a thriving nutrition and diet practice in Austin, Texas—but originally a smart-ass, wisecracking, worldly Jersey girl. If anything, she was more irreverent than me. She certainly cursed as much or more. And oh God, did she make me laugh! But she, too, was there with an open heart, and we instantly adored each other.

As Gail asked us questions, our task was to listen to one another's answers. Then, at the end of the questioning, we were to reflect back to one another the qualities in each other that seemed to stand out.

Each question Gail asked went deeper than I could have imagined. Clearly we were in no danger of ending up in skipping aardvark territory. This was amazing, powerful, deeply engaging stuff.

One query brought a favorite poem to mind by Rainer Maria Rilke, which I shared with Carly. It begins:

> *As once the winged energy of delight*
> *carried you over childhood's dark abysses,*
> *now beyond your own life build the great*
> *arch of unimagined bridges.*

Another probing question caused me to tell Carly that when my back is really against the wall spiritually, I like to think of myself as a warrior, putting on the whole armor of Love. I also shared that my favorite definition of joy is the pure and simple delight in being alive.

When we had both listened to one another for a few hours, we were given the privilege of naming each other using a compilation of the qualities that seemed to embody who we were in our truest selves. This would become our Original Medicine name. When Carly told me mine, my whole face lit up. She dubbed me the Winged Warrior of Delight.

The moment I heard my new name, I fundamentally felt its power in my heart. I absolutely felt like the Winged Warrior of Delight!

That weekend, as the Winged Warrior of Delight, I gave my first joy talk—to Gail and my wonderful new friends. It was the best Valentine ever! From myself, to myself.

The weekend held one more unexpected gift. It came from Rebecca Campbell, a young Australian woman who had flown over from London. Her first book was coming out in a few months. Bec was taking the course to become more comfortable as a public speaker, although she already had the most luminous presence whenever she spoke.

She shared her message with us: "You have an inner light within you that is craving to be shared by those around you, by the world at large—but mostly by you. When you share your unique light, bit by bit, you light up the lives of those around you. And, one by one, you inspire them to light up too. It's a chain reaction. And before long, the whole world lights up. Your light is contagious."

The afternoon we all parted, I told Bec how powerful her message of turning on our lights had been for me, and how excited I was for her to share it with the world.

"You realize, don't you," she replied in her delightful Aussie accent, "you're already out there doing it? You know what you are? You're an Undercover Lightworker!"

When Bec said that, I realized that in every talk I had been giving—whether to horror fans, design schools, or art museums—I already always spoke about joy.

I *am* an Undercover Lightworker, I thought to myself! Now it was just time to ditch the disguise and incarnate as the Winged Warrior of Delight.

⌒

In that moment I recommitted to making joy my whole focus. Since I was booked to appear the following month at Monsterpalooza, the largest horror convention on the West Coast, I had the perfect opportunity. I would create a brand-new talk about my father's legacy of joy and share with fans how joy had changed my life and could change theirs. I felt ready. So, of course, the Universe decided to up the ante.

A few years earlier, some partners and I had formed a business to promote and preserve my father's legacy. At the time, it had felt like a way of beginning to live forward my belief that spreading his joy could make a difference in people's lives. Together we began brainstorming ways to make this happen.

By the fall of 2014, however, my partners and I all realized that the financial part of our undertaking had been much less lucrative than we had hoped it would be. So we made a collective decision to work together for one more year while they got ready to move on to other ventures. This would give me another twelve months of preparing to take my "joy mission" full time out into the world.

A week after my transformational speaking workshop, I got a call from my business partners letting me know that they had an opportunity to move into another venture. They felt it was time for us to part ways sooner rather than later—as in right away. Although this was all done amicably and with great generosity, I was totally thrown. We had a big year planned and suddenly I had no financial backing for events to which we had already committed. At the same time, I recognized that this was exactly the right decision. I was simultaneously panicked and elated.

In the past, the panic would have won out. I would have chucked my newfound joy and just begun frantically looking for any way I could to make money. This time, however, having embraced my true identity as the Winged Warrior of Delight, I couldn't go back to the way things had been. Although I still upped my workload to defcon levels, I also found myself thinking about doing something that previously would have seemed as pie-in-the-sky as sliding down rainbows, riding unicorns, and dousing myself with sparkly fairy dust.

What came to me was to create a daily practice of joy.

And not someday.

Not once I had enough money or after doing everything I had planned.

Now. *Right now.*

Four years earlier, in March 2011, I had faced my misery in the mirror and vowed to change my life. In March 2015, I would take the next step: The Winged Warrior of Delight was ready to create and share her daily practice of joy! I just had to figure out exactly what that would look like.

7

MARCH
MADNESS

No one much likes March in New Mexico. It is a month of brutal winds and plumes of juniper pollen, and just as the apricot trees finally bloom, it snows. Most New Mexicans march through March in miserable moods. I was glad to be heading to Texas for work.

That's why the day of my drive to Austin seemed like the perfect time to begin figuring out what my new joy practice might look like. I decided that instead of taking the shortest and fastest route, as I usually did, I would stop at a bird refuge because birds always make my heart sing. By the time I got there, however, the day had turned hot and my pollen-filled head was pounding. I slogged through the refuge filled with more duty than joy, my nagging workaholic clock ticking in my head, and a long drive ahead. Yet somewhere deep within, I felt something familiar—like a distant mirage of joy.

When I drove on, I let joy choose my route through West Texas. A few hours later, and still far from my final destination,

I found myself on a deserted stretch of road just as the sun was setting, deep sienna loamy furrowed fields on either side of me fairly glowing in the last embers of light. Out my window, I saw a lone V of geese. Then another. Then another, until V after V of geese filled up the whole sky.

I pulled over, and as the evening sky colored from spectacular red to majestic purple to glorious gold, I got out of my car and stood there listening to the cries of thousands of snow geese seeking their nightly refuge. It was a truly magical moment. A panorama sunset of geese calling out—to my heart—which cracked open and called back to them in immense gratitude.

In that moment, I knew that I had found my joy practice. I committed to consciously and consistently connect to the wonder all around me—feeling and sharing the pure and simple delight of being alive and present in the world however and wherever it manifested. It wouldn't be easy to maintain. I had done too good a job burying joy for it simply to resurface without some serious dedication. But that day had proved to me that my connection to my own heart and to this big beautiful planet had not been, cannot ever be, extinguished.

Throughout my Texas trip, I felt as though something was being birthed inside me. In Austin, I had dinner with Carly, and we talked about our excitement for one another's journeys. In Dallas, on my lunch breaks, I found that I was seeing with fresh eyes as I walked around the neighborhood where I was working, reveling in the spring flowers. When the time came to drive home, I decided to try another joy practice. I would take all back roads—without a map.

I left Dallas, pointed the car compass northwest, and let joy lead me home.

Joy took me through towns with unpronounceable names, past abandoned cotton fields, through the increasing desolation that is rural West Texas. All the way, I went with an open heart and gratitude for my journey.

As the sun began to lower in the vast Texas sky, I listened to the audio of a class I was taking on sacred activism with Andrew Harvey and Diane Berke. At the beginning of the course, Diane had lovingly introduced Andrew as a "recovering diva." Within ten minutes of listening to him speak, I thought to myself, "Recovering? *Please . . .*"

One of the many privileges of growing up with my showbiz parents was the opportunity to meet quite a few divas—male and female. I know a diva when I encounter one. Andrew Harvey is *definitely* a diva—one whose emotional ecstasies frankly pushed every single damn one of my uptight WASP buttons when I first began the course. But that same diva ended up breaking through something no one else could have.

As I tuned in, I heard people sharing their mystical experiences with animals. I was loving this sweet exchange when Andrew interrupted, rather brusquely, "But what are we really doing here? This isn't just a lovely chat."

These lines from one of my favorite Mary Oliver poems, *Sometimes*, came to me:

> *Instructions for living a life:*
> *Pay attention.*
> *Be astonished.*
> *Tell about it.*

Suddenly I noticed a small dark cloud in the vast Texas blue sky, so small I might not have seen it had I not been paying attention from my heart. I realized it was a murmuration—a group of starlings flying together in unison—not a vast showy one, but a quiet fluid one. I prayed for the cloud of birds to fly toward me. It did. I prayed that I would catch up to it, and I did. Then just before it was going to fly away, it suddenly turned into a black liquid maelstrom that whirled down from the sky into a tree. I slammed on the brakes and stared in wonder at the formerly bare branches now ornamented with at least a hundred tiny black birds. I felt unspeakable gratitude.

An hour or so later, I found myself in Happy, Texas. (Say what you want about Texas, but it has the best damn names.) In the audiobook recording, Andrew was talking about his daily practice of gratitude, about the rapture he felt hearing an opera singer, and about gazing into the eyes of his cat Topaz knowing he was seeing the eyes of God—and so was she. Everything he said resonated.

It made me think about my father. At the end of his life, as miserably as his body failed him, my dad would always be resurrected by beauty—be it a pear in a bowl, a single chartreuse cymbidium on a pale green stalk, or a Wagner opera. He never lost his capacity for gratitude, rapture, or joy.

At that point in the audiobook, Diane and Andrew reached their final exhortation—urging us all to engage in what they called a daily practice of adoration. In that moment, inspired by the beauty of my backroads drive, I decided to begin. I would add that to my joy practice!

I was smack dab in the middle of Hereford, Texas, and I desperately needed to pee. So I stopped at a gas station and declared my intention to adore everyone I met and everything I saw.

I stepped out of the car into what I can only describe as the smell of someone taking a cosmic dump—the stench of slaughterhouses and feedlots that made the air feel almost solid. As I should have known from the name of the town, I was in the heart of West Texas cattle country. I thought, *If I can adore this, I can adore anything.*

My heart was so filled with the joy of everything I had been hearing and feeling that I did: I adored the elderly cowboy in the black hat who would have hated everything about me except possibly my famous family. I adored the dirty tattooed feet in the bathroom stall next to mine. I adored the unexpected cleanliness of a restroom on the road. I adored the toothless smile of the dark-skinned woman walking through the gas station's glass doors whose discomfiture at being in small-town West Texas probably exceeded even mine. It was amazing!

As I left Hereford on a two-lane road driving toward the setting sun, my heart started to swell in a way that words will never be able to describe—and suddenly, I was filled, absolutely filled, with gratitude for all the love I have felt in my life, both human and divine. Tears began to flood down my face.

My favorite music was blaring, which reminded me of when I was a little girl and my father would drive us through Beverly Hills. There he would roll down all the windows, turn up opera on the radio as loud as it would go, and sing at the top of his lungs—half from the joy of singing opera and half from the pleasure of seeing my immense mortification at having a father who could do such spectacularly embarrassing things in the eyes of his daughter.

Tears of adoration just poured out of me for this man who taught me what it was to love and be loved—to love people, to love life, to love art, to love food, to love adventure, to love music, to love generously, fully, and well, well, well. I sobbed and I sobbed and I sobbed. *In pure joy.*

As I drove the remaining three hours home, I thought about my resistance to Andrew at the beginning of the course and realized how that had shifted. An hour from home, I asked myself: You *used to be a diva. Where did she go? When did the 5'11" fashion risk taker become the scrawny wearer of yoga clothes? When did the irreverent mimic become the isolated homebody? When did the child whom her poet brother dubbed Merry Victorious become so somber and subdued? When did I stop being the diva iconoclast I-don't-care-if-I'm-different me— the me who felt alive?*

I pulled over and stepped out under the black bowl of a Northern New Mexico sky pinpricked with lights, splashed with galaxies, and I felt my diva come back into me—but in a whole new way. Divadom as an expression of the Divine. I threw my hands wide open and I welcomed her back as part of my truest self.

When I got home I couldn't sleep. I felt filled with an energy that I had thought might never return. I wrote these words in my journal: "A diva adores and is adored. A diva is filled with joy. Diva comes from the Latin word for goddess. A diva is divine. Though I am beyond grateful for all the dark nights of the soul I have endured (and will yet endure), for the stripping of it all away, for all the humility that I have embraced, for all the ways in which the trappings of the world mean less and less, I need to remember that spirituality does not mean always wearing my hair shirt—unless it's made of Fendi faux fur, of course!"

We are met with what we give. By cutting off my inner diva, I had cut off part of my divinity. Adoring and being adored is part of the divine equation. For the first time in what felt like forever, I remembered how it felt to be fully alive—awake and alive in joy. I felt ready to reclaim it for good this time.

8

TWISTED
MONSTERS

A few weeks later, I headed west to Monsterpalooza to unveil my new talk about my father's legacy of joy.

On the morning of my speech, I woke up feeling incredibly anxious. Outside my window, it was a sunny spring day in beautiful downtown Burbank. I looked out at the bright blue Southern California sky and felt like jumping out of my own skin. So I did what I always do when I feel out of balance. I went for a walk and prayed.

On the drive through the desert the day before, I had been listening to an audiobook by Louise Hay, one of the original motivational authors and New Thought proponents. My mind had been meandering through mile after mile of the monochromatic Mojave Desert when Louise said something that pricked my ears right up: Guilt and shame are the root cause of all of our fears and all our problems.

As I walked and prayed that next morning, her words resurfaced. I realized that the anxiety I was feeling was rooted in some very old guilt and shame. Being in Los Angeles always brings up old insecurities. That day's nasty inner monologue went something like this: *I'm not rich, successful, beautiful, unwrinkled, or brilliant. I don't even have my act together about joy. How can I go out and talk to people about joy if I'm not even able to be joyful every day in my own life?* I was flooded with fear, feeling so much guilt and shame at never having measured up to myself, let alone the standards of my hometown.

Then the thought came: We all feel fearful of being judged. The ways I am scared of judgment are no different than anyone else's fears. It may seem worse here in Hollywood, where plastic surgery and fad diets and wellness are rites of passage, but everyone everywhere struggles with the guilt and shame of never being enough. In that moment, my fear was replaced by compassion—compassion for all of us who have bought the not-enoughness bill of goods.

Although Southern California had been a beautiful place to grow up—sunshine and flowers, beaches and mountains—I never felt good enough. Despite being a movie star's daughter, I had always felt immense pressure to meet the external set of standards I believed were expected of anyone in Hollywood— of beauty, talent, and wealth. I constantly compared myself to the people who seemed to have achieved all three and despaired about my ability to be their equals. I compared and despaired ad nauseam. Comparison, I can truly attest, is the thief of joy.

Having struggled with my own bludgeoning messages of not-enoughness my whole life, that morning I prayed to stand in Love's presence, unafraid. Soon I felt a deep sense of peace wash over me. From having woken up feeling like I was going to jump out of my own skin, I felt embraced by Love.

Of course fear had come in with gun barrels blazing. I had set the intention of stepping into my new life as the Winged Warrior of Delight, a Lightworker for Joy. Fear had woken me up screaming: *Who do you think you are to talk about joy? How dare you? See, you're not joyful. You're miserable! How is that joy practice stuff going for you now?* Fortunately, the antivenom of Love had done its work—as it always does.

That evening the turnout for my talk was amazing, the response overwhelming, and the rightness of it all so clear. I felt the pure and simple delight of speaking as my truest self about something I knew could make a difference in everyone's lives.

⌒

Just in case I wasn't getting it loud and clear, however, the Universe had someone drop in for a guest appearance to further the plot of joy in the most glorious of ways.

Attending the same convention was my dear friend Sarah Douglas, an actress who lives in England. We had been emailing about possibly collaborating on some events together later in the year in the U.K. when we realized that we were going to be at the same convention. Sarah and I had been very close when I was in my twenties. Though we had stayed in touch and seen one another a few times over the years, it had been almost a decade since our last visit.

Although I was looking forward to our dinner, the prospect of seeing Sarah was also bringing up some old stories of guilt and shame. When I looked back at the twenty-something Sarah had known, I saw a self-involved, depressed, scared, self-hating young woman, constantly trying any get-rich-quick scheme.

This meant spending too much money, having all the wrong relationships, occasionally drinking too much, and despising myself for failing in everything I did. I felt nothing *but* guilt and shame about almost that whole decade of my life.

So at dinner, when Sarah began telling me about all of the ways I had helped her during that time—how the ideas, writings, and poetry I had shared with her had meant so much at that particular point in her life—she blew my mind. She told me that she still had a book that I had made in which I had hand-copied poems (some of which I had actually written myself) to inspire her. A book that she sometimes still revisited because it reminds her of her best self. I had been so mired in my ancient history of guilt and shame that I had not only forgotten that book and my own poetry, I had also completely forgotten that kind, generous, loving me.

Reconnecting with Sarah helped me to see that I had been holding on to some pretty old stories, which had built up barnacles around the clean hull of my joy. Barnacles that bumped me along my continuing voyage instead of letting me glide through the smooth and rough waters of life. Barnacles that I now could not only recognize but also remove, bringing me back home to the clear crisp joy underneath it all. That evening with Sarah was the champagne bottle cracking on that clean hull and sending it off to sail on the seas that had been calling to it for far too long—even if the voyage encounters a few tempests along the way.

9

A Rapture
of Roses

After the Monsterpalooza weekend, my plan had been to take four or five days off to write before going back to work in New Mexico and Texas. A month earlier, my literary agent had called me out of the blue and said, "I need a new book out of you." Buoyed by her enthusiasm and my new joy practice, I was ready to dive into what would be a mini writing retreat.

That Monday afternoon after Monsterpalooza, the friend in whose guesthouse I planned to write called and told me she had fallen ill—for the first time in decades. She told me I could still come, but she sounded the kind of terrible that wants to crawl in a hole and not see another human being for a week. I knew I couldn't stay there.

I decided to head up the coast to central California. I hit the road in the late afternoon, figuring I'd find a hotel room wherever I ended up for the night. Every hotel was full. It was Spring Break. For a moment, I wondered if I was going to have to sleep in my car, but at the eleventh hour, I found a hotel where I hoped I might be able to settle in and write. It was one of those uber-hip redone motels with a groovy aesthetic—along with thin walls, dirty carpets, and single-paned streaked plate glass windows overlooking a central kidney-shaped pool filled with people decades younger than me, drinking and splashing until the wee hours of the morning.

Clearly that wasn't going to work. With Google revealing not one decent hotel going for less than $400 a night, I was about to give up and head back to New Mexico when it occurred to me to check Airbnb. There it was—the perfect guest cottage high up in the Santa Barbara hills. Not only available but actually affordable!

I moved in and laid out my plans: five days of writing coupled with some long walks on the beach and nature hikes in the hills as part of my new joy practice.

For the first two days, I got up early and stayed up late. I wrote and wrote and wrote, while also ticking off other to-do's on my lengthy list. I felt so grateful to watch the words flow. But since I had also promised myself to try new joy practices every day, I also tried taking hikes and walking on the beach.

⌒

Every time I left the house to practice joy, I heard that nasty voice in my head I knew all too well saying: *What time will you get home and get back to work?*

Since I had started my joy practice, I had been trying to learn to speak kindly to that voice, given that telling it to shut up had never worked. As though reasoning with a five-year-old, I told it: *You've had a very productive day. You've worked nine hours already. You can stay out a bit longer.*

50

That sounded great—but my workaholic false self wasn't having any of it.

On my third day in Santa Barbara, I got up at 4 AM and wrote and worked for six straight hours before the exhaustion behind my eyes overwhelmed me. I decided to take a hike at a nearby botanical center. I brought my camera and binoculars to look for birds. It was as if I were watching the world from behind a gauze lens and with a leaden heart. I was there, but not present.

I felt beyond disheartened. I knew that my joy practice could work. I had felt it on those Texas back roads. But it wasn't working now.

Not knowing what else to do, I gave in and decided to get back to writing.

As I drove back to my guesthouse, a flash of riotous color suddenly streamed quickly by my window. I looped around the block and discovered the color was a rose garden in full bloom. I grabbed my camera and got out. I was hungry and tired, but I made myself go because even with a leaden heart and a blurry mind, my love of roses sang through to me. I walked through the garden with my camera, taking pictures and smelling every color.

I've always had this idea that, even blindfolded, you can tell the color of a rose by its scent. So when a young couple and I started to chat about which of the roses was our favorite, I suggested they try it—and off they went. I loved watching them holding hands, taking turns smelling each color, and sharing their observations. I had to smile.

I was almost bleary with exhaustion and hunger, but still I kept at it—smelling each color of rose and taking pictures until slowly—oh so slowly—a glimmer of hope nudged me. The butterscotch scent of yellow, the gaudy perfume of hot pink, the bittersweet melancholy of pewter. Embraced by those seductive scents in voluptuous bloom, I suddenly felt it—that tiniest flicker of joy.

Suddenly, a gust of wind rushed through the garden, sweeping hundreds of rose petals into the air and swirling them in a dervish dance above our heads. Everyone stopped what they had been doing—young couples, grandmothers with children, workmen on their lunch break, yoga moms walking their dogs. Looking up into the cloudless blue, we all let ourselves be showered with silken petals.

After that, the world changed colors. No one was unmoved by that ethereal encounter between earth and sky. Our eyes met in pure joy. A rapture of roses had transfigured us all.

I returned to my guest house lit up with joy. I felt a fresh resolve to put my new practice of joy before everything—especially work.

I had said that before. But something felt different this time.

PART TWO

STORYTELLING IN SERVICE OF SPIRIT

Do not be satisfied with the stories that
come before you.
Unfold your own myth.
—Rumi

10

WAKE UP! WAKE UP! WAKE UP!

"My name is Victoria Price. I am a workaholic."

Woken by a howling wind whistling through the Santa Barbara hills in the wee hours the following morning, I tapped those words onto my laptop keyboard.

My fingers paused.

Hello, Victoria, I imagined the readers of my words reply. *Thank you for being here.*

I paused. Looking up from the bright screen, I could barely see the dark outlines of the unfamiliar room around me. The storm outside my rented guesthouse sounded like a hundred dragons breathing fire. Like a coming army rattling their drawn sabers. A zephyr had zipped up from the Pacific, winding its way through convoluted canyons, twisting through tangled trees, to wallop at my windows: Wake up! Wake up! Wake up!

"Hello," my fingers had replied. "Hello."

Suddenly the room got very still. Outside, the eucalyptus grove crackled and moaned, rustled and raved. But the inside darkness had become my cocoon, my laptop screen my lighthouse calling me back to the shores of my own life.

I began to write.

"My name is Victoria Price. I am a workaholic. But I used to be a joyful little girl. Where did that younger me go?

"I go around the world talking about my dad—a man who knew how to give and get joy, who lived it and shared it with everyone he met.

"I go around the world telling people what I need to hear."

I stopped. Someone had turned the volume up on the storm outside. Thousands of wind-whipped brittle leaves sounded like a dissonant symphony in an orchestra playing for their lives. Their anxious arpeggio crashed into the room on a cresting cacophonous wave—into the room and into my own cacophonous heart.

I closed my eyes and invoked the words of the early-morning prayer I have spoken my whole life. I felt its benediction flood me with the hope it has always brought.

This is the day that Love has made.
Be glad.
Give thanks.
Rejoice.
Stand in Love's Presence unafraid.
In Love lift up your voice.

I opened my eyes to the beckoning screen. From deep within myself I heard:

In Love lift up your voice.
Wake up! Wake up! Wake up!
Write your truth. It's time.

I closed my eyes and listened to the storm—the one inside me. The one that had brought me to this moment. Right here. Right now. My fingers rested on the keys. Again I heard: *Wake up! Wake up! Wake up! Write your truth. It's time.*

So I wrote.
I wrote and I wrote and I wrote.
I wrote my truth. It was time.
I am still writing.
In Love lift up my voice.
It is time.

11

HITTING
THE TRIFECTA

That morning I wrote and posted my first Daily Practice of Joy blog.

I had tried blogging once or twice before, but I'd never stuck with it. Writing a book had always been my Holy Grail, so blogging had seemed like some kind of amateur literary detour.

That morning, however, I needed to let my message of joy, my fear of never moving past my workaholism, and my desire for connection through words flow out of me and into the world.

I had always journaled every morning. For more than twenty years, my core spiritual practice has been to handwrite whatever needs to surface and whatever I need to understand into my leather-bound journal. When my pen hits the paper, ideas emerge that help me make sense of my life. It is as though Truth and Love speak to me through whatever words appear on that blank page. Each day I write myself whole again.

That's what that first Daily Practice of Joy blog felt like—and what each one of them has felt like ever since. After four years of talking about joy and then falling back into the morass of workaholism—rewind, repeat, rewind, repeat—I only really began living a joy-based life after I posted my first blog. I could never have known that sending my truth out into the world with the simple press of a button would so radically change my life.

I had no expectations for my blog. I just knew that if I kept ignoring my own heart and silencing my true self, one day everything would irreparably shatter. The whole time I was in Santa Barbara, I couldn't stop thinking about my dear friend Dee, who had lived and died a few hours up the coast from right where I was staying. In the four years since her death, a day had not gone by that I did not think about how much I loved and missed her. When I wrote that first blog, I felt Dee right over my shoulder—this soul friend who had so supported my dream of writing that she had bought me my first computer. I felt her urging me to finally show up to my truest self and stop listening to the bludgeoning voices of self-doubt. "You can do it," she assured me, as she had so often when she was alive. "I know you can, you know you can, and God knows you can. God and I are right here with you. Live your life whole."

From my very first blog, I took the risk of revealing parts of myself I had never thought I would let anyone see. I wrote about my fear and failings, my hopes and dreams, my delusions and desperation. It felt unbelievably scary airing what my mother would have called my dirty laundry. But I had finally recognized that I couldn't change my life by myself. I had to create a community of fellow joy practitioners—even if I only imagined them in my mind.

Right from the start, I risked one more thing that felt huge. Along with writing about my daily practice of joy, I shared what had become one of my go-to joy practices—photography. That felt especially vulnerable. I had always loved photography, but I'd never thought of myself as anything but a hobbyist. To "publish" my photographs felt both terrifying and true. It meant that I was choosing my love of doing something creative over my fear of never being good enough.

That first blog served as my promise—to myself and to anyone reading it—that I would never stop practicing joy every single day and then sharing it with everyone I met. What I didn't expect was that what I was writing would resonate with so many people. I ended my first Daily Practice of Joy post with this quote by Henri Nouwen: "Joy does not simply happen to us. We have to choose joy, and keep choosing it every day." Not only did I choose joy that day, as I have every day since then, but I began connecting with people all over the world who were also willing to choose joy. Step by stumbling step, we began resurrecting joy together.

⌒

When the idea had come to me to create a daily joy practice, I was simply following my heart-based hunch that showing up every day in joy was the key to shifting my lifelong battle with workaholism, lack of self-worth, crippling doubt about my life purpose, and even the biggest monster of them all—self-loathing. I had no proof that this would work, other than I knew that I always *felt* better—about myself, about my life, about my purpose, about others, and about the whole planet—when I moved through the world with joy.

As it all turned out, it did work. Practicing joy and sharing my practice changed my life, shifted my addiction to work, allowed me to stand up to my lack of self-worth and reduce my doubts about my life purpose. It has even gone a long way to heal that lifelong lie of self-loathing.

It took me until my fifties to finally show up to my truest self and begin living my best life. So what worked when so many other things I had tried hadn't?

Three things in combination: Joy. Practice. Accountability.

I embraced my own joy and committed to showing up to it every single day by practicing it. Practicing it so I could get better at it.

Then—and this was the kicker—I held myself accountable to others in my sharing of my joy practice. Accountable to my own creativity. Accountable to my desire to heal—both myself and others who were struggling in similar ways—through sharing the words that came through me. Accountable to a new community of fellow joy practitioners.

Joy. Practice. Accountability.

Those three things changed my life.

⌒

How did that happen? To be honest, I made it all up as I went along.

If joy evoked in me the pure and simple delight in being alive, the first thing I had to figure out was how to practice delight.

I had to stop talking about joy and begin experiencing it. Then I had to keep doing that—over and over again, every single day. No matter what.

That's how I created my daily practice of joy: I began showing up and practicing the pure and simple delight in being alive.

But none of that practice would have amounted to a hill of beans without accountability. I had to share my practice with others in a way that finally honored the creativity I had spent decades burying under layers of fear, self-doubt, and workaholism. Not only did I have to practice joy, I had to invite joy out to play with others.

That's been my trifecta: Joy. Practice. Accountability.

Although I had found the winning formula, putting it into place wasn't always easy. Even my best friend, Pamela, thought I was nuts. When I sent her my first blog, she said, oh so helpfully: "You're going to write about joy? You're miserable! Shouldn't you wait to see if it works?"

Sometimes the people closest to us get so caught up in our stories that the narrative prevents them from imagining another way. Pamela is now my biggest cheerleader—always reflecting back to me how my life has changed since I began my practice of joy. But when the vision of those near to us becomes as myopic as our own, we have to find other resources. I found exactly the encouragement I needed in the words of Quaker educator and activist Parker Palmer.

Palmer wrote, "I've never written a book on something I've mastered . . . I write about things that feel to me like bottomless mysteries—and I start writing from a place of beginner's mind. For me, writing . . . begins with making a deep dive into something that baffles me—into my not-knowing—and dwelling in the dark long enough that 'the eye begins to see' what's down there . . . Novices are often advised to 'write about what you know.' I wouldn't call that bad advice, but I think it needs tweaking. Write about what you want to know because it intrigues and baffles you."

Parker Palmer gave me all the permission I needed to dive deeply into the joy that had so long both intrigued and baffled me.

Every week though—and trust me, it happened every single week—my false self came up with some very convincing excuses for not practicing joy: too busy, too anxious, no inspiration, the dog ate my joy. I heard them all! Then I remembered that I had to write a blog and share my practice with others. So I just kept at it, kept practicing joy, every single day. Every Sunday morning, I wrote my blog.

Sometimes my practice wasn't pretty or my blog particularly delightful. More of a wrestling match than an Ode to Joy. That's what practice is. Sometimes the shot goes over the net, sometimes it goes over the fence, but if you keep doing it long enough, eventually it not only goes over the net, it goes for a winner. You keep at it, and pretty soon you don't want to miss a day—even the days when the number of balls on your side of the court far outnumber the ones on the other side.

I have kept practicing joy every single day. I made the commitment to *myself* to wake up every morning with the conscious intention to experience and celebrate the pure and simple delight in being alive. Then, successful or not, I have shared my practice—boils, bumps, bogs, elation, ecstasy, excitement. I have shared it all.

⌒

At first I felt a little like a cross between Bill Nye and Harriet the Spy. I sleuthed my own life to find clues about the things that brought me joy and then tried to create the perfect environment where my petri dish of joy could grow.

I began at the very beginning. I started by simply giving myself permission to be more childlike. I laughed at my dogs. I really did stop and smell the roses. Making my morning cup of tea or watching the sun come up out my bedroom window made me feel a kind of immense pleasure I had forgotten was possible. When I heard something new or even something I hadn't remembered I knew, I let myself feel it and say, *Wow!* I meant it.

I splashed in puddles, left dishes in my sink, binge-watched episodes of my favorite childhood TV show—*I Love Lucy*. Whenever I didn't know what to do next, I dug deep, past all the accumulations of adultness that I had thought were supposed to be me, and found that joyful little girl and asked her what *she* wanted to do next.

But guess what? Misery missed my steady company. She clamored for my attention. She told me that this was way too easy, that joy needed certain things—things that she reminded me were in short supply: the right bank account balance, having time off, certain people who were no longer there.

My false self nattered on at me:

This would have been so much easier if you hadn't lost everything.

Imagine the joy you could have had with actual money in the bank!

Joy would be so much easier if you could just take a vacation.

Remember how much joy you felt laughing with Dee.

If your dad was alive, you wouldn't have to practice joy. You'd just feel it.

Mostly, however, misery wanted me to believe that I needed possessions—possessions that, after my life had fallen apart,

I no longer had or could afford without going into debt to buy. My father's joy, as it all turned out, often came with my mother's shopping list of cars and clothes and gadgets that were guaranteed to make me feel happier.

I kept at my sleuthing and my science experiment. When misery told me that I needed something to feel joy, I went below the actual thing to the feeling I had about the thing—the feeling I had had when I used to have the thing. I transformed things into thoughts.

Like horses. Until my year of following in my dad's footsteps, the most joy-filled time in my adult life had been when I owned, rode, and bred horses.

It had been my childhood dream to have my own horse. In my thirties, before my financial crash, I finally got to live my dream! Misery wanted to tell me that after my life had fallen apart in 2006 and I had lost my horses, I had also lost my joy. Misery made a very convincing argument that unless I got my horses back—I would never really feel true joy again. So even though my horse friends always reached out and asked me to come ride with them, I never did.

When I started my daily practice, I decided to stop wallowing around in that old familiar it-would-be-better-if-only slough of despair and figure out what it was about that time that had made it so special.

One particular memory kept surfacing. I was at a tiny weekend horse show in Rifle, Colorado, a one-stoplight town just off the Interstate between Glenwood Springs and Grand Junction. The stables and the arena were run down; there wasn't a restaurant or a decent motel for thirty miles. But all around were the massive peaks of the Rocky Mountains underneath an indigo Colorado sky.

I had been up early that morning to help muck out stalls and groom horses with my friends. By the time I finally got on the back of my beautiful palomino, Sundance, who had a glorious mane down to his knees, I was a little tired as I rode over to join the other horses in the well-worn rodeo arena that had been designated as our warm-up pen. Sundance and I walked, trotted, and loped for a bit, then we moved to the center of the arena to stand. It was part of our practice. Standing still and being present right where we were. Together, just the two of us, connecting our bodies and our hearts and our minds.

Sitting on Sundance's beautiful back, looking up at those majestic mountains all around me, surrounded by my fellow horse lovers, I heard myself say to me, *If you had told me when I was a kid that this was how I was going to get to spend my weekends, riding horses with my friends in the Rocky Mountains, I would have thought that I was going to be the luckiest grownup ever. Wow! Look at my life. I really am the luckiest grownup ever.*

Although I lost so many things after 2006, I realized I didn't need to lose my gratitude. In gratitude, I could *still* be the luckiest grownup ever! By transforming my thinking about those old stories of loss, I was able to remember not only my love of horses, but also how much I need connection.

Joy cannot flourish in isolation. As I conceived and created my daily practice of joy, I began to find connection again—sometimes out in the world, sometimes in the pages of a book, sometimes in song, but always in my own heart. Like the magic words of my childhood, joy got me where I hoped to go.

12

THE GALAXY
OF LOVE

The more I began sharing joy, the more my life began to change. I noticed it everywhere. In work, in play, in speaking, and in writing. Even on the phone when I am tempted to get testy with a customer service person, if I connect through joy the result is inevitably joyful. Joy, I've discovered, always begets joy.

Remembering my joy; deliberately practicing it every single day; and being accountable to myself, to my creativity, and to the sharing of joy became my transformational trifecta. But what if somebody didn't feel the same way that I did about joy? Could they create a similar trifecta combining their own magic word with practice and accountability?

I began thinking about my fellow transformational speaker Bec. Her book, *Light is the New Black,* had come out and was a bestseller. Reading it, I realized that what I describe as my joy practice, Bec describes as being a lightworker. In our speaking course, the immense light emanating from her when she spoke connected to the joy in me. Joy and light recognized and communicated with one another—and from there, they emanate love and hope out into the world. The words were different, the feelings not entirely the same, yet the results were identical. We were both shining.

That, I realized, was the key!

In order to shine, each of us has to figure out what turns on and powers up our inner lights. When we do, *that* is what we have to practice, daily and deliberately. That is what we must remain accountable to within ourselves and with others. In my life, that power source is joy. Joy shines through me and connects my heart to the hearts of others. But I wondered what other people's power sources might be. So I started brainstorming in conversations.

I began by describing how joy makes me feel: Joy is my sweet spot. When I am in joy, I shift out of my head and into my heart. Sometimes it feels like my whole heart is lit up from the inside out through joy. Only from my wide-open heart can I then connect to others and the planet and the Universe. Joy is my connector.

I shared how joy always shifts me out of darkness and back into light: When I am mired down and can't seem to lift myself up, joy always works where nothing else can. It's my reset button. It takes me back to the essence of who I am and makes me feel my inherent wholeness. Only from that place of wholeness can I help others feel more whole themselves.

I talked about using joy as my litmus test if I don't know what to do about a situation: When my mind can't give me the answer, I just need to remember to check in with myself and see if whatever I am doing or saying or even considering evokes joy. That tells me where I need to be present. It also reminds me how.

As I described my relationship with joy, people always lit up. They nodded and smiled, saying they knew exactly how I felt. Then they began to share their power sources, sweet spots, and reset buttons: Love, connection, compassion, creativity, balance, awe, groundedness, surrender, inspiration, wonder, passion, loving-kindness, hope, faith, equilibrium, and reverence were some of the qualities people shared.

Anthony is a hairdresser. He is a total people person. He loves talking to people, sharing experiences, being with others. He comes from a big extended Italian family in Connecticut. Now that he lives on the other side of the country, almost every vacation he and his partner take involves large groups of family and friends. Connection turns on and powers Anthony's light.

When I met Karen, one of the first things she told me was that her father used to say, "Everything in life comes down to balance." That seemed pretty abstract until I got to know Karen better. The thing I have come to love most about Karen, and the thing she came into my life to teach me, is balance. No matter Karen's struggles—and she works a very intense and often disheartening job—she is rarely out of balance. She always finds a way to keep her equilibrium. She weighs the hope in equal measure to the heartbreak, the love to the fear, the humor to the horrifying. I love how it feels to be around her, and so I've tried to find more of my own balance in everything I do. Balance is Karen's reset button.

Anne gives possibly the best hugs in the whole wide world. I used to be a teepee hugger. You know, the kind of person who hugs you with their head and arms only—keeping the rest of their body as far away from human contact as possible. I come to that naturally. My mom was a world-class teepee hugger. My stepmother was even worse. Hugs were a barely perceptible feint toward one another followed by a few half-hearted air kisses. It has taken me years to feel safe enough to really hug and be hugged. Sometimes I'm still a cautious hugger. But not with Anne. You just can't be cautious when Anne hugs you, because when Anne hugs you, it feels like you are completely safely totally embraced by Love. So when Anne told me that her power word was Love, I was not at all surprised. She said she sometimes feels like she's been put in the world just to love people.

"Yup," I replied. "You sure have. You live Love, and your secret weapon is your hug!"

When I explained this idea to my best friend Pamela, she told me that she didn't need a word. Instead of a word she had a feeling—a feeling beyond words. "Exactly!" I said. "But this is a book. You have to write a book with words."

Pamela is my spiritual workout buddy. She has taught me that isolated spirituality is really a contradiction in terms. Pamela and I either walk or talk almost on a daily basis—and those walks or talks are our church. It's just that sometimes our church looks a little more like WWE matches than peaceful prayer. So as we were debating about the necessity of words, she said, "It's only when I surrender to something beyond words that I get where I need to go."

"Surrender! *Bingo!* That's your word!" I felt it the moment she said it. Like me, Pamela struggles with relinquishing control. Surrender connects her back to her heart and to her Higher Power.

In the early years of our friendship, whenever Pamela was twisted up in knots about something, I used to try to fix her. As soon as I understood that what Pamela always needed was to surrender, I realized that the best thing I could do was also to surrender. Instead of trying to fix her, I just needed to listen and love her. Whenever I do that, she always calls me a few days later and says, "Thank you for listening and being there with me. I finally got to the place of surrender and everything shifted. I feel like me again."

One of the words I love most is *namaste*: "The divine in me sees the divine in you." That's what joy does for me, connection does for Anthony, love does for Anne, surrender does for Pamela, and balance does for Karen—they bring us back into connection with the divine in us that sees the divine in everyone and everything else.

When I look up into the vast night sky, out beyond the nearest constellations I can glimpse an immense web of light, reminding me that all of us here on this tiny blue-and-white marble are part of a bigger whole—each of us an essential luminosity in the divine tapestry. We are all stars—and only when we know what lights us up can we shine. Only when we shine can we experience life as our truest selves. Joy makes me shine. Joy is my power source, my native tongue, my magic word, my heart connection, my reset button, my litmus test, my sweet spot, my inner star. It is all of those things, because joy is the language in which I am encoded to recognize, extend, and express all the love and good that I came here knowing were my birthright.

When we know our magic word, we know what lights us up, and then we can shine. We are all stars in the Galaxy of Love.

If each of us has our own unique way of shining our lights, I knew that to shine mine I had to write this book. But to do that, I had to stop listening to a very strident voice in my head. This voice had always told me that I talked too much about all the wrong things to all the wrong people. This voice always tried to prevent me from speaking my truth. This voice told me silence is golden. Sit down, shut up, be still.

Although I now understood that this voice did not belong to my truest self, I couldn't stop myself from tuning in to its litany of lack. I had been listening to it for as long as I could remember. To let go seemed inconceivable.

This was my mother's voice. To keep writing and sharing my joy, I had to uproot the old stories I had inherited from her.

13

THE STORIES
OF OUR LIVES

I come from a family of gifted storytellers.

My mother's stories painted vivid pictures in fascinating detail, which often led to a life lesson she hoped I would learn. My dad had a genius for tossing off scintillating stories that allowed people to feel like they got a glimpse of his soul. Both of my parents' stories were always laced with good humor and generally peppered with a dash of self-deprecation, before sending their listeners off cradling a bit of wisdom we felt grateful to have gleaned.

In the introduction to my biography of my father, I quoted Adrienne Rich, who said, "The stories of our lives become our lives." As a public person, my father perfected turning his life into sound-bite stories for the press and his fans. He told those stories so often and so well that the stories themselves came to seem as much his life as anything he had actually lived.

Aren't we all writing our own true and not-so-true stories? Story upon story upon story, all of which eventually find their place in the his-story of humanity. It's when we start to over-identify with our stories that we begin to lose the thread of truth. Our stories begin to matter more than our actual experiences.

Our stories are not us, however. We just think they are. When we spend our whole lives fictionalizing the false self we want the world to see, we become more focused on other people's opinions instead of showing up in our authentic vulnerability as our true selves.

So what happens to the real us underneath our stories? Our truest selves? We hide them. In fact, we hide them so well that, when we need them, we can't find them—like that spare hundred bucks we all put in a "safe place" for a rainy day that we can never manage to find when we need it.

When my rainy day finally came in 2011, I needed to hunt down that hundred bucks of the hidden real me that I almost forgot had ever existed—because as happened with my father, the stories of my life had become my life. To live a joy-filled life, I had to learn to get lost to those stories that were never mine. To let them go.

Problem was, I liked my stories. They felt safe, managed, and familiar. To release them felt anxiety-provoking. Yet each time I did, I remembered my true self.

I needed to begin to write a new story. In order to do that, I had to find my own voice, separate from the voices of my larger-than-life parents.

After all, I grew up as the child of two people who were widely regarded as role models and inspirations. People thought of my parents as a Hollywood power couple—my father a Renaissance man, my mother a creative innovator. I was raised to follow in their footsteps. I was given lessons in everything, the best schooling, and the opportunity to experience the world through travel. But from the time I was young, something else kept calling me. I ignored it because it spoke far more quietly than the razzle-dazzle of the outside world. I felt called to find a way to do something that gave back to the world. I know now this was the voice of my true self urging me to live out from the heart of Love.

As I began to create and then blog about my daily practice of joy, I began to connect with other people in hope instead of withdrawing from the world in shame. Blogging joy invited me to initiate a conversation about all the sweetness and the sorrow, elation and anxiety, faith and fear we all face every single day. At last, I had begun to engage in the kinds of healing, transformative conversations that I have been waiting my whole life to have.

Creating a daily and deliberate practice of joy and being accountable to it plugged me back into my divine Source as my truest self. Joy lit me up from the inside out. Any time we shine our lights, the whole world gets brighter. Underneath all the darkness, fear, anger, and doubt we all feel every single day, our true selves are longing to shine.

I have begun to think of myself as a storyteller in service of Spirit. In every exchange, my goal is simply to speak true, because each time any of us speaks our truth, we give others permission to do the same. To speak true is to speak from our hearts in the language of Love.

Nevertheless, after the initial elation of my joy practice, I began to hear those old familiar voices again—always telling me something discouraging, disheartening, or downright depressing. They bludgeoned me with the same old stories of lack and not enough—money, love, creativity. It began to feel like every joy was followed by a concomitant joy kill. That's when I realized that, along with creating a daily practice of joy, I also had to commit to facing down each and every joy kill I encountered.

Anyone who has flown much has likely encountered the dreaded air traffic term "low ceiling"—a low cloud layer that makes it hard to see the sky above, the ground below, the runway, the runway lights, and especially other planes. After I took off into my joy practice, for a few months it was mostly fair weather and smooth skies. I thought I had it made! Then fear lowered its cloud cover right onto my joy.

As a little girl, I had been taught in Sunday School to remember that even when all we can see is clouds, the sun is still always shining. God is Love, even when we don't seem to feel much love. As an adult, I have often recalled that simple idea when life feels more dark than light. But this new fear onslaught didn't feel like a layer of clouds that would soon blow away. This felt like that dreaded low ceiling: I couldn't take off, I couldn't land, I couldn't see.

I had hoped that my joy practice would allow me to soar away and leave all my old fears far behind. Unfortunately that's a Disney movie, not a spiritual journey. Although each new practice we create gives us more tools with which to deal with the low ceilings of our lives, in order for the clouds to lift, we must invite the winds of change.

It can feel almost impossible not to get lost when you are surrounded by clouds so low that you cannot see anything around you. Pilots who are not instrument-rated are not allowed to fly in this kind of weather because everything in their body lies to them. They go up when they should go down; they lose the ability to correctly determine their body position in space. Their perception of the direction they need to fly can feel so far off base that it may end up in direct contradiction to reality. They have to learn how to fly by their instruments instead of relying on their body and their eyes. They have to defy everything their body is screaming and trust that the gauges of their airplane are speaking true.

It's the same with us. We have to lose our faith in our old ways of being and instead learn a new way of flying.

When I began my daily practice of joy, I was so sure I had found the way out of my ongoing boom-or-bust cycle of misery and hope. In my excitement about remembering my joy and practicing it every day, I had forgotten one of the fundamental spiritual paradoxes: To find our truest selves, we must be willing to go by many ways we do not know in order to get lost to the comfort of our old accumulated identities. Only by embarking on this often bewildering and always unfamiliar path can we begin to come back home to Love. This path is the Way of Being Lost.

One of my go-to books on the Way of Being Lost has been *Dark Night of the Soul* by Gerald May. He has helped me see—over and over again—that "maybe, sometimes, in the midst of things going terribly wrong, something is going just right." Remembering that when you're in the middle of a dark night, however, can be unbelievably hard.

Gerald May believes we *must* go through many dark nights of the soul in which we expunge our old ways of understanding everything—including, or perhaps most especially, our relationship to the Divine. He writes that most of us "have made an idol of our images and feelings of God, giving them more importance than the true God they represent. We easily become so attached to feelings *of* and *about* God that we equate them *with* God, and thus we wind up worshipping our own feelings. This is probably the most common idolatry of spiritual life."

⌒

It is said that our childlike feelings about God are formed by what we feel from and for our parents. The image and likeness of the Divine in which we believe ourselves to be created comes in large part from the way that Love is expressed to us through our own mothers and fathers. Because we arrive in the world expressing love and expecting only good, we are naturally first drawn to those people who exude love and good. For me, that was my dad.

In my Sunday School, I learned that God is Father Mother Love, both maternal and nurturing, paternal and protective. I now know this to be a pretty radical idea. Most other churches in the 1960s would have thought it heresy. For many, the Christian God is still the God of Michelangelo, a muscular, white, bearded man in robes who can create the world through the power of his index finger and send lightning bolts down to destroy us all.

Although I was fortunate to grow up learning that God was Father Mother Love, to me God always felt like Father, because my father equaled unconditional love. My mother, on the other hand, meant love all tied up in strict morals, firm rules, and human perfection. Standards that tripped me up and made me afraid I would never be good enough. Father God made me feel safe, seen, and understood for exactly who I was. Father God was joyful, generous, forgiving, fun. As a child, I modeled God and myself on the person I adored most and whom I knew adored me. My dad.

As my mother's authoritative messages found more of a foothold in me, however, my ideas about God gradually morphed into more of a Moralizing Mother God. That false god was really just fear in fancy clothes (who, if my mother had anything to do with costuming her, would always have been attired in tasteful pumps and the perfect little black dress). That Moralizing Mother God was awfully good at her job, forever holding my feet to the fire. Barking her inner fear monologue in my ear, her One Right Way ruled my life.

I know now that my mother created her One Right Way to assuage her own deep spiritual anxiety—her own fear that she would never be good enough for God. All of her religious rules, rituals, and regulations were meant to assure her that if she followed them, everything would be OK.

Although I resisted, resented, rebelled against, and reacted to all of those rules, rituals, and regulations, I also assuaged my own spiritual anxiety with that same One Right Way. Like my mother, I wanted to believe that all I had to do was to dot all my religious i's and cross all my theological t's to get to heaven.

Reading Gerald May helped me see that I needed to begin to let go of my own need for easy answers and pat assurances. On the Way of Being Lost, I had to become willing to go through many dark nights of the soul and learn how to free fall into grace. Each dark night has helped me see that every difficult relationship, every financial hardship or disaster, every creative failure or spiritual wrestling—all the things that have felt so hard at the time—have actually been beautifully right. Each time we experience another dark night of the soul, they become less and less scary. Instead of harrowing experiences, we can see them as necessary rites of passage.

Instead of fleeing, we can learn to welcome them.

In fact, I have come to think of struggle and failure not as a pejorative, but as a building block for the soul. Every experience that has taken me to my knees in fear, guilt, and shame has become an opportunity for me to witness and so choose to lose another life-limiting old story that has ceased to serve me.

Once I realized that my daily practice of joy would be equal parts sharing joy and facing down joy kills, I had to learn to find joy in both. I had to begin to trust that even when fear lands us up in the darkest places of our lives, we are being led toward the Light. When we are willing to bring our old stories into this Light and let them be transformed by the healing power of Love, we can learn to live in new and transformational ways.

As human beings who are hardwired to learn through story, how we tell the stories of our lives has the potential to change how we hardwire our world. By deciding to become a storyteller in service of Spirit, I finally found a way to be of service to something larger than my own self-interested narrative.

This is the life work in which all of us who hope to heal our planet must be willing to engage: By exhuming, expunging and erasing all that no longer serves us and so removing the blocks to Love, we are not embarking on some personal salvation mission to make our own lives a little bit better or happier. That self-help scenario is often just another smokescreen thrown up by the small self desperate to keep running our show. By letting Love revise our internal narratives, we are not just rewriting our own stories. We are becoming the Wikipedia of the world—contributing to a powerful new narrative of hope, wholeness, and healing.

PART THREE

EXHUMING THE UNHOLY TRINITY OF MY SELF-LOATHING

*Love sometimes wants to
do us a great favor:
hold us upside down and
shake all the nonsense out.*
—Hafiz

14

REMOVING
THE ASTERISK

To the outside world, my life has looked like a success. I have done reasonably well in the movie and television industries, in the art and design world, and as a public speaker and writer. What the outside world doesn't know is what woke me up that morning in the mirror in 2011: I had never shown up to the life I imagined myself living, because I never really believed I deserved to succeed at anything I genuinely loved. Instead, I coasted through most of my life being good enough at things that were merely good enough.

Guess what? Good enough is just a backwards version of not good enough.

The question that plagued me was *Why?*

Why have I copped out on myself over and over again? Why haven't I given my all to do the things I wished I could be doing? Why haven't I allowed myself to believe that I deserved to do the things I love most?

To answer those questions, I had to take a good long hard look at the patterns of my life that had consistently taken me away from what I loved and made me become a past master at shoulding.

The answer is always, in all ways, the same old same old: fear.

⌒

I am a huge sports fan! In sports, there are certain players or athletes who have done extraordinary things but whose achievements or records will always be followed with an asterisk. A long jumper whose record was wind-aided, or a home-run king marred by allegations of steroid abuse. Asterisks are permanently attached to their names.

That's how I've felt for far too long. Like I have an asterisk following me.

As a little girl, I was told that I was God's perfect child. The loved of Love. But not because I was some special case. We *all* were God's perfect children. We *all* were the loved of Love. I fundamentally believed that everyone, including me, was perfect, whole, complete, beloved!

When I was about five years old, I came flying out of Sunday School to meet my mother, eager to share what I had learned that morning.

"Do you know why the lions didn't eat Daniel when he was in the lion's den?" I asked her.

She shook her head no and smiled expectantly.

"It's because they were God's perfect lions," I told her.

Her face broke into a huge smile.

"I love that!" she said to me, genuinely delighted. "And you know what that means, don't you?"

"What?"

This was the kind of conversation I loved to have with my mother. I adored it when she got lit up by an idea and her whole face shone with joy. Most of the time, she seemed so tense and overwhelmed by her life. These were the moments I cherished.

"It means that Puffie is God's perfect pug, Pasquale is God's perfect poodle, and you are God's perfect child!"

After that, we always used that expression. At first, it felt joyous and full of promise. As I grew up, however, something started to change. When I did things that were imperfect, as all children do, my mother always said: "I am trying to remember that you are God's perfect child, even if you aren't behaving like one." Every time she did, I felt both terrible about myself and totally confused.

I kept trying to wrap my head around her words. How could I be perfect if I was capable of acting so imperfectly? How could God's perfect child keep doing things that caused such anger and disappointment? Suddenly God's perfect child started to seem like something I had to do, something special to try to be, instead of who I just inherently was.

My mother's image of who she wanted me to be seemed hopelessly at odds with the ebullient rough-and-tumble mostly fearless child I was. My hair never stayed glued to my head. My shoes always came home scuffed. I showed up late and got excited about all the wrong things. I chose to ride the horses that threw me over the fences. I never wanted to eat what was on my plate. I read too much but studied too little. Mostly I talked far, far too much about all the wrong things to a lot of the wrong people in all the wrong places.

On the heels of my mother's increasingly frequent pronounce-ments of my imperfection, three things happened: My mother ex-plained all the logical reasons why my behavior was unacceptable. My mother punished me for that behavior. My mother sent me to see a wide range of people whom she hoped could help me be more perfect in every area of my life—from math tutors and dance in-structors to therapists, orthodontists, and spiritual practitioners. Perfect, I eventually came to believe, always seemed to be defined by someone else. Who I actually was—a good kid filled with all the typical childhood enthusiasms and impulses—was clearly not perfect in the way I was expected to be.

Although I still felt like I was the same me I had always been, more and more attention was being paid to this imperfect me that I seemed to be becoming. What had been viewed as endearing excitement or funny rambunctiousness when I was little seemed increasingly problematic as I grew older.

When I was a little girl, every night I prayed the same prayer:

God loves Mary Victoria Price.
And Daddy and Mommy and Barrett and Rini.
And the birds and the fishes and the turtles and the animals.
And Paisley, Pasquale, Prudence, and Puffie (our assorted dogs, whose names all began with P).

Then I'd name all the other grownups I loved. The list went on. But it always began with me: God loves Mary Victoria Price.

I believed that—until my mother's definition of perfection, along with her airtight disciplinary system hell-bent on enforcing that definition, began to change me. I started to feel further and further away from the Mary Victoria Price who God loved. Slowly but surely, all the focus on what I was doing wrong began to whittle away at my fundamental belief in my own rightness. The love and good that used to seem so natural slowly morphed into qualities outside of myself that I had to earn or achieve.

School didn't help. Our educational system is a meritocracy. We are taught to work hard to get good grades so we can get into the right colleges and go on to have successful careers and supposedly happy lives. There were some students who did this really well, while most of us were hit and miss. Of course, there were others who *really* lagged behind. Over time, we all came to know where we stood in that hierarchy and that we would all get our just rewards. Except that those rewards weren't so just after all.

I bought into all of that for the longest time: I wanted to succeed. I wanted to be rewarded. I wanted to prove my abilities. But somehow who I was didn't always match up with who school wanted me to be. I seemed to constantly end up in the principal's office for doing something that seemed to come very naturally: talking. I was just connecting in joy with my friends, but that joy seemed to be disruptive to my teachers. I loved my teachers. I didn't want to be rude—but my enthusiasm didn't mesh with the decorum required in the classroom.

My troubles at school affirmed what my mother told me at home. I began each day expecting my own inherent goodness to shine through. By the end of the day, those easy expectations had often been tarnished by things I had done or said that caused anger, disappointment, or irritation. I was imperfect.

I began to wonder whether someone up there had gotten the script wrong about me because God's perfect child didn't seem much like the child I actually was anymore. God who loved morphed into a more mercurial God who meted out merit-based rewards and punishments.

I wondered: *Could this God still love me even though I was so imperfect?* I knew my mother and father loved me, and my teachers liked me. I also knew that everyone wished I could learn to rein myself in. I believed that they and God would love me more if I could behave better.

Deep down, though, I never stopped knowing that Love loves everyone in the whole wide world unconditionally, no exceptions. I believed that with my whole heart in the same childlike way I had always believed it. Nothing could touch that. Nothing ever has. So that reward-and-punishment system in which I was investing—try harder to be better, to be less imperfect, and so succeed in the world—seemed to apply only to this imperfect me living inside a divine demerit system.

Eventually, I just took imperfect into my own hands. If I was going to be a fuck-up, I might as well do it with flair. I became an iconoclast, a weirdo, a creative oddball. I excelled at the things that I enjoyed and scoffed at the things I didn't. I followed the rules that made sense to me and flouted the ones that didn't. When I got detention for breaking rules that seemed ridiculous, I ditched detention because I thought that was ridiculous, too. I also became best friends with many of my teachers and aced all the standardized tests. I got into all the right schools and received the awards I hoped to get. I seduced people with my potential but then showed them that only I would choose what I wanted to do well. I became known as that artsy rebel at whom no one could ever seem to get too mad because even she knew she was playing a big game.

Underneath it all, I felt like I was failing. Failing God, failing my mother, failing my teachers. Deepest down, I felt like I was failing me. I had stopped believing in my own goodness. Either I was rebelling, resisting, resenting, and reacting, or I was failing and falling on my face. I was so focused on other people's ideas of me that I stopped listening to my own heart. Fear had taken the reins.

Eventually my core belief devolved to this:

> *God loves everyone in the whole wide world.*
> *No exceptions.**
>> ** Except for Mary Victoria Price.*

That sounds funny, I know. It didn't *feel* funny. It felt dark, disappointing, a little bit dangerous, and completely disillusioning. For a long time I stopped expecting the best of myself. I stopped trying to succeed at anything I loved. I gave up on me.

That all changed when I committed to creating my daily practice of joy. That was the first time that the adult me wholeheartedly chose Love over fear.

Did fear just lay down its weapons and applaud my return to Love? Hell, no. Fear was not about to give up its cushy position and pension plan that easily. That's why every time I identified a new joy practice that inspired me to believe I could live the life of my dreams, fear immediately dive-bombed me with its joy kills.

Their message was always the same: *So you think you deserve a joy-filled life? What makes you think that you can have the life of your dreams? Who do you think you are to have anything to offer the world?*

That old asterisk kept rearing its ugly head, so one of the biggest tasks that I had to face in creating my daily practice of joy was to identify exactly how that nasty asterisk had come to attach itself to me in the first place, to unearth its deeply entrenched beliefs, exhume them, and so finally erase that nasty untrue asterisk from my record.

Doing this isn't just about finding and forgiving our human imperfections. Living with our old stories and our supposed limitations will never take us back to the clean page that we truly are. We have to find a way to see beneath the lies the world has told us and we have believed, in order to return to the fundamental truth of our own goodness and lovability. We have to stop being so focused on our mistakes, our scars, and our life-limiting narratives. No matter how the asterisk attaches itself to any of us, no error can ever make what's true untrue. What is true is that we are all fundamentally, inherently, and irrevocably good and loved. Period. The end. No asterisk.

After I began my daily practice of joy, three old stories from childhood began surfacing and resurfacing in my thoughts. These seemingly inconsequential incidents from my past screened themselves onto my consciousness over and over again until I could no longer ignore them. What were they trying to show me? Could they be the source of my asterisk? I had to invite Spirit to tell me what I needed to learn from these old stories.

I heard my answer: I needed to be willing to dig deep enough to exhume these old stories and bring them up into the light of day. To let go of a lifetime of fear-based shoulds, I had to be willing to become a dispassionate but loving anthropologist of my own past.

In a childhood of extraordinary privilege encapsulated for posterity in photo albums of travels and encounters that any child or adult would have envied, a childhood filled with far more joy than sadness, with opportunities that opened the kinds of doors most people never even know exist—a childhood that seems mythical even to me, the one who lived it—these three minor moments stayed with me for reasons beyond what seems logical or explicable. Moments to which I have returned over and over again, like touchstones—to pull out and hold, to examine and explore—before putting them back to rest in the bottom drawer of my memory. Moments I have never forgotten, but whose import I never fully understood, as though they were preserved on film in a language I could no longer comprehend. Enigmas in my own history that held clues to some essence of me that kept calling me back to myself.

When I began unearthing old joy kills, these three moments began coming to mind with such regularity that I knew I was being invited to explore them. At first, I wasn't sure if how I remembered them was how they had actually transpired. Eventually I realized that knowing whether something happened exactly as we remember it doesn't really matter. It's what we *do* remember of what happened that is significant. Memory is a notoriously fickle friend, sticking around when we want it to leave, leaving when we are desperate for its company.

Memoirist Patricia Hampl believes that we don't write what we know—we write in order to find out what we *don't* know. In the blankness of the blank page, we can feel both our confusion and our hunches about what might have happened. Hampl helped me see that "We only store in memory images of value." Of value to *us*.

To write ourselves whole, we *have* to question why certain memories and ideas and images and beliefs keep screening themselves up from our subconscious onto the surface of our lives. We have to discern their value to us so they can become part of our healing.

That sounded great on paper. But when people I shared these anecdotes with kept asking, "What did you feel?" I didn't know how or even if I wanted to know. In the end, that became my first real clue: These relatively insignificant incidents kept scratching at my surface precisely *because* I felt something that, even as a little girl, I knew better than to let myself feel. I had buried my own feelings about what had transpired. It was those unacknowledged feelings calling out to me.

As I began to allow myself to feel what I had not felt then, I came to realize that each of these three minor childhood moments had eroded something pure and innocent and true in me, leaving behind a little girl who no longer fully believed in her own fundamental goodness, wholeness, and potential. On the outside, she looked like the same confident little girl everyone thought her to be. On the inside, her sense of self-worth had been replaced by her belief that she was wrong, problematic, not good enough, undeserving, and bad.

Just as I had sleuthed and scienced my joy practice, I had to do the same for my joy kills. Once again, I found my clue in the word "should." Anything I had done in my life because I thought or had been taught I should usually was the culprit.

Shoulds are shapeshifters. They morph into whatever form it takes to get us to ante up to their pot. Shoulds always make us feel separate from Love. Separate is the root of the whole problem: the idea that we're over here, someone else is over there, and all of us are separate from Love that we feel we have to earn. Our good gets buried under our shoulds. Remove the should and you always find the good.

15

BEVERLY HILLS BRAT

"Do you know what a Beverly Hills Brat is?" my mother asked, seething.

She had just careened across two lanes of traffic on the hairpin curves of Sunset Boulevard and slammed on the brakes as soon as we reached the safety of a side street. She never took her hands off the steering wheel, yet I felt as though she had grabbed me by the scruff of my neck.

Of course I knew what a Beverly Hills Brat was. They were the boys who actually believed they deserved the privilege they had been born into—without having to prove their self-worth to themselves, their parents, or anyone else who might be watching. The girls, who, without doing anything but be their perfect selves, made me acutely aware of all the ways I felt inferior and unlike them, down to the white-on-white saddle shoes I had to wear because my mother believed I couldn't stay between the lines polishing the black-and-white ones I wanted.

A Beverly Hills Brat was someone who felt entitled to the gifts they were given, often at the expense of others.

"I will *not* bring up a Beverly Hills Brat! Do you understand?" She didn't have to raise her voice to make her intentions crystal clear. "Don't you *ever* say or even *think* anything like that again."

I nodded mutely.

The reason for my mother's rage? I'd hoped to get a part in the school play, and I had made the fatal flaw of enthusiastically telling her that I probably would get it "because of dad."

Those three words came out of my six-year-old mouth without thought. Three words that changed everything. Three words I could never rewind back to the childlike place of innocence and enthusiasm that produced them. Three words I have feared would define me forever. In a sense, they have.

Because of dad.

~

When I said "Because of dad," what *did* I mean? Was it something sweet: Because my dad was an actor, they would think I could act, too? Or something Beverly Hills Bratlike: Because my dad was famous, I expected to get what I wanted?

My mother never asked.

Because she didn't ask, in my memory I skipped over my own internal narrative of the story and continued on with the plot of what happened next. When our garnet-colored station wagon hurtled across those lanes of traffic, I knew I must have said something really, really wrong to provoke such an unsafe response from my mother, who was usually such a cautious driver that she often drove around a block to avoid making left turns across traffic. Was I scared? A little. But I was used to being a little scared by my mother's frequent pronouncements of right and wrong in her dualistic, moralistic world.

My mother saw herself as a definite woman given to making definite pronouncements about anything in which she believed strongly. *Definite* was one of my mother's favorite words. *Definite*, in the vocabulary of Mary Grant Price, meant you knew what you believed and you weren't afraid to do or say it. Mary Grant Price knew Right, she knew Wrong, and she was determined that her daughter would, too.

Definite in my own vocabulary, and that of my friends, equaled strict. Strict meant that what other kids were allowed to do, I usually wasn't. Strict meant getting *no* for an answer when my classmates usually heard *yes*. Strict meant having to stand up straighter, get better grades, turn down invitations to cool stuff, or hear a long lecture about why I shouldn't behave like the other children.

My best friend Casey had a mom like mine. We talked constantly about how strict our moms were. (Actually, we just talked about everything constantly, which is why I spent so much time in the principal's office.) Our moms were elegant, well-spoken, beautifully mannered, well-coiffed, powerful, talented, thin, and strikingly attractive women who were married to very famous men. Unsurprisingly, my mother and Mrs. Cole admired one another greatly.

Our mothers ruled our lives. But Casey had one advantage over me. Not only did she have siblings, but she also had her twin sister, Timolin. Like so many twins, the two of them have a deep, unbreakable bond. Many years later, when we were in our early thirties, Casey suddenly said to me over lunch one day, "You know Timmy and I used to wonder how you survived without anyone to talk to. We always had each other, so we could figure out what seemed crazy and what didn't. You didn't have anyone but you."

Until Casey said that, I had never really thought about the way my mother's definite pronouncements had landed on the childhood me: My mother's beliefs felt like holy edicts, cardinal rules, perhaps to be questioned, possibly even occasionally disobeyed—but never without knowing I would pay the penalty for my transgressions.

Although my mother spared the rod, she did everything else not to spoil her child. But more than the pronouncements or punishments, what really got to me was her disappointment. Rebel though I might have seemed, all I really wanted to be was good. Don't all kids want that, deep down? I wanted to do right—but to my mother, that meant doing it my mother's One Right Way.

By the time the Beverly Hills Brat exchange happened, I was used to my mother's definite points of view and her impossibly high standards for me. I knew what awaited if I didn't bow in obeisance to them. So I wasn't necessarily scared of what my mother might do to me if I acted like a Beverly Hills Brat. But I was definitely scared—because the instant my mother uttered the words "Beverly Hills Brat," she gave voice to my deepest fear about myself.

What if I really *was* a Beverly Hills Brat?

I felt ashamed, mortified, that I could ever have thought something so selfish, so wrong, so, well, Beverly Hills Bratlike.

Worse, I was afraid that if I could think it, I could be it. I could become one of those girls who made others feel less-than, insecure, unworthy.

It was one thing to feel different, odd, quirky, uncool, unlike the other kids in ways that I couldn't even articulate to myself. It was another thing to be a jerk.

The net effect of my mother's admonition has been that I have spent my whole life being nice, humble, and hardworking in order to prove to myself, to the mother who still lives in my head, and even to the larger world that I am *not* a spoiled Beverly Hills Brat. That hasn't been a bad thing on the surface. It's what happened underneath that has had a lasting deleterious effect by fundamentally changing how I thought of myself. My mother's teaching moment made me afraid that I couldn't expect good from myself because I actually might not *be* good. That was the most terrifying thing I could feel. Until that moment, I had thought that good was my fail-safe. That was the moment the asterisk landed on the beautiful blank white page of me.

Once I understood that as an adult, everything came flooding back to me. I knew with utter clarity that when I said "because of Dad," I didn't mean "because I'm more special than other people are because my dad is a famous actor." My class was full of kids of famous people—Clark Gable's son was in my class, and his dad was probably the most famous actor in the world. I literally meant *because* of Dad—because I felt, with the purest of childhood joy, that *everything* I wanted to do was because of Dad! Of course, that would include acting.

In other words, what was really the most innocent and joyful of remarks—said from the pure sweet place of loving my father—was transformed into exactly the opposite, something nefarious. This old story was my foundational joy kill—the original moment when I stopped expecting good from myself and instead embraced the lie of never good enough. That moment seeded in me a lifelong fear of not-goodness, of not-enough-ness.

We all have these kinds of stories. Until we can root them out of our subconscious, we all walk around believing in our not-enough-ness. These are the stories that underlie all of the difficulties we face over and over again throughout our lives. They are our weak spots.

When a dam breaks, the water always bursts through at one place first. Not because the water puts more pressure on that spot, but because that's where the dam is weakest. That's what happens with us.

Fear breaks through where we are weakest. Not because we came here with inherently unsound places. Not at all! These are usually the weak, fearful, unworthy places we have unconsciously inherited from those who raised us.

I learned my fear of being not good enough from my mother. My mother's moralizing messages took root in her own old stories of inadequacy, of not being good enough. Having grown up in the colonial British caste system, aspiring to be something better than her birth status, my mother immigrated to America to forge her own creative path in the world. Which she did! My mother was an extraordinarily creative, strong, interesting, brave, successful, accomplished woman. Her fears, however, inherited from her own parents, immigrated with her.

What were my mother's fears? The same as her mother's. Of aspiring to something better, yet not believing they were good enough to achieve it. That was difficult enough . . . and then my mother entered the world of celebrity—where good enough is never, ever, ever good enough. Where being better, thinner, funnier, smarter, more beautiful, more talented is all that matters. Celebrity coupled with a religious and emotionless British upbringing that brooked no whining and in which discipline was king led Mary Grant Price to live by standards that were utterly unachievable on any human plane—and yet which she expected herself to maintain. Her fears of not living up to those standards ruled her life.

Those fears became amplified after she had me. Fear of being judged for her own self-identified flaws cubed by her fears of being judged a permissive mother of a Beverly Hills Brat.

Her anxiety about how she might be seen, because of what I might become, felt palpable within me. Her fears took seed in the fertile soil of that younger me, and there they grew. Throwing out tenacious roots that attached to everything that mattered, wrapping themselves around anything that might be called ambition, strangling the enthusiasm of joy, and eventually becoming that bumper crop that seems to sow itself in spades in so many of us—the epidemic of modern humanhood—shame.

Alongside my mostly self-confident, almost always enthusiastic, generally competent, adventurous, funny, joy-filled true self grew the insidious twin of my false self who began to whisper nasty little nothings in my ear. She urged me to doubt myself, reminding me of all my little failures, stockpiling shame and self-doubt, changing my expectations of myself, of my creativity, and of the world—from self-loving to self-loathing. Eventually I became a workaholic in the unconscious hope that my perpetual busyness might keep the deep unworthiness I felt at bay.

If feeling my mother's fear sowed the seeds of my shame and self-doubt, and workaholism became the way I sought to stave it off, then perfectionism was self-loathing's slave master. This was yet another of my mother's complicated legacies to me: The Absolute Belief in the Possibility of Perfection.

Perfect is just one-third of a very tricky trio: The Three P's. Even if you've never heard of them, you have probably experienced them: perfectionism, procrastination, and paralysis.

Perfectionism means taking on a set of impossibly high, utterly unfulfillable standards and then believing that our task is to accomplish them, which sets ourselves up to fail. That's when our subconscious comes to the rescue in a very dodgy superhero outfit called procrastination.

Knowing we can never reach the ridiculous heights to which we have been told we should aspire—and fully believing that aspiring to those heights is the only way to live—we procrastinate in order find ways to avoid failing.

Who are we failing? For me, it began as my mother. But at some point, my mother's impossibly high standards became my own. I expected myself to do, write, dress, act, say, pray, love, eat, feel, *be* . . . perfect. Faced with my inevitable failure to be a revolutionary off-the-charts genius spiritual creative wunderkind, I procrastinated to the point of eventually giving up.

Eventually the dance of perfectionism and procrastination leads to a near-fatal condition in our personal, creative, and spiritual lives: paralysis. It convinces us to bail out on our dreams—immobilizing ourselves as creative or spiritual or relationship or physical or life failures. When that happens, we spiral into shame. Shame is the secret sauce that takes us from feeling we're simply a low-grade loser to becoming a full-on self-loather.

⌒

When I first heard about Brené Brown, I was immediately struck by the courage it must have taken someone in academia to *choose* to be a "shame researcher." Even Brown admits, "When I use the word 'shame,' people have one of two responses: I don't know what you're talking about, but I'm pretty sure it doesn't have anything to do with me, or I know exactly what you're talking about and I don't want to discuss it with you." Brown breaks shame down into the two-headed monster with which I'm pretty sure every single person in the Western world has at least passing acquaintance. Shame, she says, "drives two primary tapes: not good enough, and who do you think you are? Its survival is based on us not talking about it, so it's done everything it can do to make it unspeakable."

I am fairly certain I am not the only person who has spent far too much of my life ticking off items on Brown's terrifying list of shame: "Perfectionism, judgment, exhaustion as a status symbol, productivity as self-worth, cool, what do people think, performing, proving, quest for certainty, fear of creativity." Been there, done and felt them *all*!

That's why letting not good enough in the door is such a big deal. The moment we expect not good enough, shame has found its toehold. Whenever we try to take back our good to shine our lights, shame yells out loud and clear so we and everyone else can hear: *Who Do You Think You Are?*

Before I began my daily practice of joy, I heard that *Who Do You Think You Are?* practically every single day of my life. It is only recently that I have begun to take back that question from shame and ask it a different way.

What if "Who do you think you are?" meant this: Who do you think you *really* are underneath all the messages you've been given?

In my heart of hearts, did I really think I was or could ever be a Beverly Hills Brat? No! But once fear convinced me that it could be true, I built up a wall of niceness and false humility that I hoped could help me not to be the Beverly Hills Brat I always fundamentally knew I wasn't.

This was the birth of my small self, who kept convincing me that I needed to try to be someone I already knew I could never be. In other words, I have lived life as a double negative.

Now my true self is turning shame's screaming question on its head. Instead of believing there's some Shame Committee out there made up of all the people we think do life better than we do (the cool kids, the gurus and healers, the ridiculously creative people, everyone we place on a pedestal) who are looking down on us in disapproval, we can all learn to ask ourselves: Who do we think *we* are?

Posing the question this way—from the inside out—the answer always feels different. When I trust that I am still that me who came onto this planet as a joyful, good, loving little girl, then I am listening to my true self. She lets me answer with my whole heart: I think I am who I was created to be, who I came here being. I came here as joy and good, and I still believe that is who I am. I'm not some sorry person trying to be perfect, because it's not about human perfection. It's about being our truest self.

I did not have to be nice to prove I wasn't a Beverly Hills Brat. I *was* nice.

I did not have to apologize for not being good enough because I hadn't lived up to my mother's expectations of me. I just had to be the good I already was.

I did not have to be ashamed of all the ways I had failed or might fail others. I just had to show up in the Love that was my birthright. That Love just loves.

I was not, nor had I ever been, a Beverly Hills Brat.

I was, am, and will always be, God's perfect child.

I just had to have the courage to keep exhuming, expunging, and erasing those old stories that never had been mine in the first place in order to find that my truest self had always been waiting for me to return home.

From that beautiful, sweet, true place, I was ready to unlock the mysteries of the other two childhood incidents that kept surfacing.

16
MY BLUE PERIOD

It was a special treat to be picked up from school early and brought home to change out of my flannel grey uniform into my favorite dress, the white one patterned with tiny pieces of fruit. For my mother, attending school was sacrosanct. I had started nursery school at two and kindergarten a year later. I never missed a day. So to be going to an art opening on a weekday afternoon meant something very special . . . and we were going because of me! My bright blue finger painting had been chosen to be in a show of paintings by kids from all over the city. I was four years old.

Perhaps I was acting excited, but more likely my mother had her speech rehearsed. Undoubtedly she and my father had discussed it, along with, I imagine, a joke or two about this being my Blue Period. Of course, I can't know that this happened but I can hear it in my mind as though it did—their perfectly matched, wry, wide-ranging intellectual humor and their well-meaning laughter at my expense.

My mother's proclivity to worry and her need to moralize—the maternal desire to protect coupled with the British imperative for restraint and knowing one's place—made this a teaching opportunity. One which, if passed up, might lead to further heartbreak for me . . . or worse, contribute to my becoming one of "those" children, the kind who took their privilege and place in the world for granted. I often wonder what my dad had said to her—whether he suggested that she not say anything at all, or as he often did during their fights about my table manners or finicky eating, if he just deferred to her moral authority.

In the dressing room next to the high counter where my mother laid out my colored ribbons, she brushed my hair back into the tight braid that always accompanied me out into the world, pulling my skin so taut that my eyelids seemed to stretch. Truly not a hair was out of place, as though this were the one part of me she could even begin to try to tame. Then she knelt down and looked me in the eye as she said: "You need to know that you were not chosen to be in this exhibition because you show any particular talent as an artist. They chose your painting because they wanted Dad to be there. Your father and I don't want you to get hurt later on, so we need you to understand this now."

I have no memory of feeling anything when she said this. The photo of me taken an hour later standing next to my dubious monochromatic masterpiece (indeed entitled "Blue Period") does not depict a devastated child. There is no sadness in my eyes, but there is no particular joy either.

To the world, my mother presented herself as creative, competent, and controlled. However, I always felt the depths of her fear and had the perpetual urge to protect her. Despite my innate desire to mother my own mother, however, to question her authority felt scary. I chose to take what she told me to be truth because I needed her to be right. Like all kids, I wanted my mother to translate the world and make it safe. I had to believe her.

That moment stayed with me because I took her at her word when she told me I was not good enough. I could suddenly see that my painting never would have warranted being chosen on its own merit. *Of course* it was my father they wanted and not me. I internalized that dispassionately and clearly, even at four.

It's not what or even how people impart things to us as children that creates their lasting mark on our psyches. It's where those things come from in the people teaching us and, consequently, how those things land in us. The way we feel—empowered or dismayed, encouraged or disheartened—weaves itself into the narrative tapestries of our lives.

The adult me now knows that this is no way to talk to a child. I could rewrite that moment a hundred ways, most of which would have left out the conversation altogether. Yet I feel neither rancor nor animosity toward my mother, nor even much sadness toward some loss of innocence in myself. No. This is why it stuck: That afternoon, I was told that I was not good at something that the person I loved most in the world (my dad) valued and adored more than anything (art). Vincent Price may have been best known as an actor, but his greatest passion was visual art—an avocation we would come to share as I grew older. I also learned that anyone—even me, in our Hollywood movie-star life with a world-famous father and a seemingly omnipotent mother—could be used as a pawn in the game called celebrity, a game I was just beginning to understand existed.

From her own place of not good enough, my mother never thought to find a way of pointing out the positive—both in my creative effort and in my having been included in such a prestigious show. Instead, her words made me doubt myself. I did not deserve to be there. I felt unqualified, untalented, and out of place.

I know now, just as I knew then, that she never wanted me to feel not good enough. She just wanted me to see that any feelings I might have of privileged specialness might end up hurting me down the line. I needed to see the man behind the curtain in the Oz called Hollywood! Since then, I always have. For that, I will always, always be grateful. But what stung—and so what stuck—was losing the freedom to be creative simply for the joy of it.

Instead, I decided that I needed to find something that would make me good enough to be chosen some day. In other words, I stopped expecting my own creative good—however it manifested—and invested myself in trying to find something outside myself that others would deem worthy.

From then on, with every one step forward in my creative life, two steps back have always followed. Instead of creating from my heart, I let my head tell me what to do. Which really means I stuffed Love in the trunk and let fear drive the car on this road trip of life for far, far, far too long.

⌒

A few years after my dubious art debut, in one of the after-school art classes I continued to take, I was painting a small oil canvas of an Old English sheepdog, inspired by the TV show *Please Don't Eat the Daisies*. I could *not* get the painting to turn out the way I wanted it to—and finally I had to ask the teacher, Mrs. Davis, to help me finish it. I watched as she turned an expressionless blob into a sweet dog visage. In that moment, I decided that what I saw in my mind would *never* come out of my hand. It was my final affirmation that my mother had been right. I really didn't have any artistic talent. It was one of the defining moments of my childhood. I was seven years old.

As children, if we are told that we can never be good enough at something, we take that as carved in stone. Some part of us gives up on that quality in ourselves. Whereas if we are encouraged to believe that we can improve at something, we continue to practice and persist. When we are told that there is something we cannot do, in the moment we believe that pronouncement we are robbed not only of our present joy but also of all our future joy in that endeavor.

We come to believe that the only people who succeed do so because they have natural gifts. If we feel we do not have those same gifts, we then search for an area in which we do. Instead of following our hearts, pretty soon all we are trailing is the red herring of externally sanctioned success. We try things that other people find success doing, because they are rewarded and we want to be rewarded, too. We are doomed to fail, because we have stopped knowing who we are and have begun listening to anyone but ourselves. When we do fail, however, we take it beyond personally. Failure feels permanent. Fatal.

Sooner or later, we give up on our passions and start following the breadcrumbs of good enough our parents or

115

teachers or peers toss out: *You're good at math, but you're no Einstein. Try accounting.* That is our excuse to stop trying to do what we love. Eventually we travel so far from our true selves that we can no longer remember them.

When I accepted my mother's statement, not only was my belief that I could become an artist tarnished, but so was my joy in even trying. I couldn't shake the idea that I would never be good enough at anything truly artistic.

There were three areas of my parents' lives where their burden of fear seemed to outweigh their own fundamental expectation of good. Unsurprisingly, those are the precise areas that have speed-bumped and road-blocked me: money, creativity, and privilege.

Both of my parents always feared that the next job, film, or creative project could be their last, and then the money might run out. Therefore, they could never rest on their laurels. The blessings of their lives needed to be garnered through humility and hard work lest they be taken away. Privilege must be earned, never expected.

Both also valued art/design more than anything in the world, while they themselves felt unworthy and untalented as artists. Growing up, my father dreamed of becoming a painter, but in high school he decided he could never be as good as the artists he admired, so he studied art history instead and eventually became an actor. Yet he drew and painted beautifully throughout his life—privately, just for himself. As successful and beloved as my father became as an actor, he would have given anything to be a Modigliani or Matisse. If he couldn't match up to his idols, then he would succeed at something else.

My mother became a costume designer because she did not think she was good enough to become a Martha Graham dancer. Her closest friend at the time was Merce Cunningham, who went on to be one of the most famous dancers of the twentieth century. She judged herself against him and imagined only future failure. She turned to costume design and quickly rose through the ranks of Broadway designers, working on some of the most famous musicals of the Golden Age of Broadway. Yet she derided herself constantly for what she saw as her chief failing—the inability to draw as well as her colleagues. Never mind that her reviews were extraordinary, or that one of her sketches graced the logo of the Costume Designers Guild.

We pass on what we have not healed. My parents' fears were transmitted to me, and I am still scraping their residue off all of the creative areas of my life.

That's why deciding to share my daily practice of joy through both writing and photography was such a huge deal! Blogging gave me the freedom I had never felt to write from my heart. By posting my photographs, I was not only giving the finger to the messages from my past, but I was actually saying that what I enjoy matters more to me than anyone else's ideas of talent. I could almost feel the years of disappointment in myself slough off of me.

Psychologist Angela Duckworth says the grit that it takes us to succeed at something we love entails four things: interest, practice, purpose, and hope. When it comes to my creative life, I have plenty of the first three. It's the hope that's been the whole problem.

What I lost that afternoon when I was four was hope.

I became a teacher, an art dealer, a designer—all creative artistic professions. I wrote magazine articles, television episodes, and my father's biography. But I never had the courage to lay it on the line to show up to the heart of my two truest creative passions—writing and art—until I began to share my practice of joy. Then, finally, joy gave me the courage to override fear.

The word courage stems from the French word *coeur*—heart. To find courage, we first have to find and delete those life-limiting narratives about all the reasons we cannot, should not, must not, and will not. We must rewrite our own stories from our hearts.

During Picasso's famous Blue Period, he used an almost monochromatic palette of blues to depict the misery of the human condition. Wanna know what came after the Blue Period? (Picasso, let's face it, knew a thing or two about change.) What came after the Blue Period was the Rose Period.

When I began my daily practice of joy by allowing myself to express my creativity freely through words and photographs, it was time, at long last, to bid adieu to my all-too-lengthy Blue Period and don my joyous rose-colored glasses. By identifying the joy kills that caused me to squelch my own creativity, I could release them—not with regret, but in gratitude for everything they have taught me.

Knowing that it is *never* too late to live the lives we have always known were ours to live, I finally embraced the creativity of my truest self. Just two years after summoning up the courage to share my photographs in my blog, I even had my first solo photography exhibit!

That showed me that I was finally ready to hear what the last message from my childhood had to tell me—so I could let that old story go, too.

17

My True
Inheritance

Sometimes I feel as though most of my youth was spent as a passenger in my mother's car while she cautiously negotiated the surface roads that crisscross Los Angeles like capillaries between the clogged main arteries that are the Southern California freeways. She prided herself on knowing the best shortcuts and which streets had the most consistent stoplight timing.

At first she took surface streets because she believed they were faster. Later, she developed a phobic fear of freeways that prevented her from ever taking one again. This meant that trips that might take other people 30 minutes could take my mother and me an hour and a half. During that time, we had countless conversations about many, many topics.

When she picked me up from school or from the bus stop, my mother would request a detailed rundown of my day, reminding me that if she was going to chauffeur me around, I needed to entertain her. No checklist of events for her—she wanted a story with precise details, down to the color hair ribbons people wore, moments of dialogue, and what I imagined a person felt when they'd said something.

This day was different. *She* had a story for me.

She had edged our station wagon out into the left-turn lane by the fire station on the corner of Sunset and South Beverly Glen, a street I loved because of the towering sycamores shading the picture-book houses, each representing a different geographic style—clapboard Colonial, Southern colonnade, and my favorite pale yellow one with white wooden shutters like the family home where Elizabeth Taylor lived in *National Velvet*.

"Do you know what inheritance is?" she asked the eight-year-old me, checking the oncoming traffic flow once again and edging a bit further into the intersection.

"No."

"It's what you get when someone dies." She stepped firmly on the brake pedal and glanced over at me. I must have looked perplexed, because I wasn't sure what you would want to get from a dead person.

My next thought was, *Who's dying?*

The traffic finally petered out, and she made a cautious sweeping left and drove on under the sycamores.

"This is what you need to know," she stated evenly, firmly, but with a vibrating emotion I could feel underneath her dispassionate words: "I don't believe in inheritance, so you won't be getting any from me when I die."

That was the end of the conversation.

When my mother made pronouncements like Never Wear a Plaid without a Dominant Color or Always Live in a Home with a View, I was always left to figure out for myself that plaids without a dominant color were too uniform to be visually interesting. Rich people with good taste lived in homes with views. So it was with the inheritance pronouncement, which like the others was repeated when necessary to be absolutely sure that I heard it.

This one was just a lot tougher to parse because I never really understood why my mother would not want to give me, her only child, an inheritance. But I had to make sense of it, because clearly she felt very strongly about it. And it was never going to change.

This is what I came up with:

✢ Children should never just be given money for no reason, unless they are spoiled. I don't want to be spoiled.

✢ Money is something that must be earned. I will earn it.

✢ Other people control money—not me—and those people determine who gets it by who deserves it. I must not deserve it.

Once again, what I might have heard as a mere idiosyncrasy (my mother's disavowal of inheritance running curiously contrary to most of the rest of the world) or something that seemed grossly unfair (why shouldn't I get what other kids have?), I ended up taking as an indictment of myself. My lack of self-worth to be reflected in perpetuity in my lack of net worth.

My whole life I have always been able to bring in money. What I have never been able to do is to keep it. If what we experience in our lives is the external manifestation of what we believe, I have never believed that I deserved to be supplied. That's what I was told when I was little. That's what I have always held to be true. In one way or another, I have frittered all my money away because I did not believe I deserved to have it in the first place. When things fell apart and I lost everything in 2006, I believed that I deserved to lose everything.

Over my lifetime, I have made a lot of deals with a lot of devils. Not human devils—my own. Sure, some of my own devils may have looked like my partners in life, love, banking, or business. But they weren't. They were me projecting my own complete lack of self-worth out on the movie of my life and watching the plot play out on an IMAX screen for everyone to see. This is why, every time "someone else" screwed me over, I never did all the things people wanted me to do—namely call them out or sue them. *This is my fault,* I thought. *I promise to work harder and make it all better.*

It wasn't until I began exhuming these three old stories that something clicked: I realized that all the hard work in the world wasn't going to heal what was broken or what was making me broke. What was broken, in every way imaginable, was my belief in myself as someone who could never expect good or live in creative abundance.

Unless I could learn to believe that I deserve to do what I love and be paid well to do it, I would be doomed to Groundhog-Day my financial life forever. A perpetual cycle of boom and bust, earning and spending, amassing debt and paying it down. Over and over again.

Until that conversation with my mother, I had never heard the word "inheritance." The eight-year-old me had no idea who paid for or would continue to pay for things as my life went on. I had never thought about that. I took the roof over my head and the food on our table for granted.

When my mother told me that although other people got inheritances, I would not, I accepted it. I knew it was another of her Teachings on the Perils of Privilege: Entitled children who do not know how to make their own way through the world become entitled lazy adults. But it also landed on that place in me already fearful that I might not be a good enough person to deserve good things.

My mother was terrified that money would bring out the worst in me: The Beverly Hills Brat. I knew I didn't want that! Now, of course I know that plenty of people raised in great wealth and privilege have gone on to make extraordinary contributions to the world. Then, I just heard it as one more thing to be afraid of—in myself.

⌒

Over the years, I have come to understand more about both of my parents' financial beliefs. When people ask me what scared Vincent Price—the man who scared everyone else—my pat answer is always snakes. The only time I ever saw my father utterly terrified was when I accidentally stepped right over a nest of baby rattlesnakes. That blanched expression on his face is the look I will always associate with pure terror. But the real answer to what scared Vincent Price is actually money.

My father's financial angst was his only real Achilles heel, as far as I could see. The one chink in his otherwise invincible joy armor. He was afraid of having money, but also afraid of not having it.

My dad often told the story of his grandfather, Dr. Vincent Clarence Price, a multimillionaire and household name in the nineteenth century as the inventor of baking powder and the head of a huge food empire. Dr. Price had, according to my father, "lost everything" in the Panic of 1893. When I delved into my family history while writing my father's biography, however, I found out that the cataclysmic losses my dad had described weren't true. Dr. Price had lost a lot of money, as did many wealthy people during that market crash, but he had not ended up in the streets. What *had* happened was that he had pulled his youngest son out of Yale and put him to work in one of the family businesses.

That son, also Vincent Price, had dreamed of becoming a poet. Instead he became one of the most successful candy makers in the United States. He had two sons. His oldest, Mort, wanted to become a jazz pianist. Like father like son, Mort was put to work in the family business. Eighteen years later, when his youngest son and namesake Vincent wanted to become an actor, he had softened. My grandfather not only encouraged my dad's dreams, but initially he also helped bankroll them by giving his youngest son a check for what it would have cost to become a member of the local country club. My grandfather then forbade him to use that money for anything but following his creative dreams.

My father always felt such guilt that he had been allowed to do what his equally artistic and creative older brother had not. He assuaged that guilt by working as hard as he could over a 65-year career. He prided himself more on being a "good provider" than a good actor. He also carried the fear that if he ever lost all his money like Dr. Price supposedly had done, he would have to give up on his own dreams and get a "real job." I know that argument all too well. It's the one my false self has used on me over and over again. Like my father, I have always halfheartedly pursued my dreams while running in terror from the perils of poverty.

My mother had grown up all over the world with parents who believed more in protecting their social status than in providing their children with anything but a roof over their heads. Her father teetered perpetually on the brink of financial ruin. At one point they lived in China with a houseful of servants. Five years later, the family found itself in rural British Columbia living in a rudimentary log home, barely making ends meet. Unlike my father, my mother had great confidence in her ability to make and manage money. Her fear was that she would never have enough of it or that it would run out. She believed that the only way to assure that you could be supplied was to work as hard as you could work to outsmart the system. She was always one step ahead of the game, even if she had to be a bit "creative" doing it.

What they both had in common—despite their immensely privileged lives—was their profound fear of lack, so common among that generation that lived through two world wars and the Great Depression. I was raised in that amniotic fluid of scarcity.

I filtered my mother's no-inheritance edict through the filter of the financial fear I always felt from both my parents and I began living their legacy of lack forward. By high school, I never got my weekly allowance, because if I neglected one thing out of twenty on my list of chores, my mother gave me nothing. Instead of renegotiating the deal with my mother at fifty cents a chore as opposed to her all-or-nothing five dollars, I told myself that I didn't deserve it anyway.

When I began to create my practice of joy and commit to following my dreams, I knew it was time to revise those old narratives of scarcity, lack, and fear.

It hasn't been easy. On the Way of Being Lost, I have lost far more money than I have gained. I never know how I am going to pay my bills, and yet they always get paid. I never feel like I have enough, and yet I always have plenty. I am terrified of not having a roof over my head, and yet I always have a place to sleep. My financial life continues to be the final frontier of my fears.

As I've been purging more and more old untrue tales about scarcity and lack, however, each new fear that surfaces feels less daunting. Even when my heart is beating out of my chest in some ancient anxiety manifesting in some new fresh financial fear, I now have more and more faith that I can find my way back whole.

That's how we heal: After a river has frozen into ice, it's hard to remember that it ever was water—especially in the depths of winter. Spring thaw usually comes slowly. Day after day the sun shines, and the ice begins to melt a little. Night after night, the temperatures drop, and everything hardens up again. It's easy to wonder if the ice ever will melt. Then one day it just cracks and floats away. Or that's how it seems. Actually, it was all the days of sunshine, all the frozen nights, and all the slowly warming temperatures along the way that transformed the ice back into the river it had always been.

PART FOUR

MISSING THE MARK

*There is a sacredness in tears.
They are not the mark of weakness,
but of power.
They speak more eloquently
than ten thousand tongues.
They are the messengers of . . .
unspeakable love.*
—Washington Irving

18

HEART OF STONE

I was born into a family of WASPs to an English mother who firmly believed in the merits of a stiff upper, well, everything. For my mother, emotions were not comfortable. Excessive celebration was impolite. Crying was flat out forbidden. My mother believed that crying meant you felt sorry for yourself, and that feeling sorry for yourself was unconscionable. My heart, I learned at a young age, was never a safe place to linger.

Shortly before she died, my mother told me a story that brilliantly illuminated the effects of her child-rearing philosophy: When I was five years old, she and my father and I were walking through an airport. A couple came up to us. This was not unusual. People were always coming up to my father. These two, however, happened to be our neighbors—though we had never met them. They lived behind our house on the top of a small hill. We could not see their house, nor they ours, which was how folks liked it in our wealthy Holmby Hills enclave.

After exchanging a few niceties with my parents, they looked down at me and said, "Oh! You must be The Screamer!"

At first both of my parents looked confused, but then the penny dropped for my mother. She was mortified. My bedroom was at the back of our 9,000-square-foot house, and when she or my nannies put me to bed, I began to cry the moment they left.

As so many parents of that era had, my mother took much of her parenting advice from Dr. Benjamin Spock, who believed that if a mother continually gives in to the cries of her infant, the infant will "realize after a while that he has his poor, tired mother under his thumb and he will become increasingly disagreeable and tyrannical in demanding this service." So both my mother and the nannies left me to bawl and eventually scream myself to sleep. They got far enough away not to hear me, but apparently our poor neighbors did not. I imagine that their cocktail hours were rather unpleasantly accompanied by my caterwauling, which is how I became The Screamer.

In retrospect, what I find most interesting is that my mother shared the story with me at all. Did she regret her decision, or was it just a humorous tale to her? Probably a bit of both. For me, it was a clue into my early emotional life.

In infancy, I learned that crying was never going to elicit the response for which I hoped: being held, being loved, not being abandoned. The few times I was tempted to cry when I got older, my mother explained why crying made me seem spoiled, self-centered, and ungrateful. I didn't want to be that kid. I stopped crying before I turned four. It was easier to close down my heart and not feel anything than to feel afraid and never find any human consolation.

~

I kept up my stoic front even when my father fell in love with his *Theatre of Blood* co-star, the British-Australian actress Coral Browne and I found out that my parents were getting divorced.

When my mother discovered that my father had been having an affair with Coral, she was devastated. But she was willing to do whatever it took to keep their marriage together. It was my father who asked for the divorce. That flattened my poor mother. They had been married for twenty-three years. They were more than husband and wife, they were creative partners. She later said to me, "We had always been on the same team. That's what broke my heart."

Nonetheless, when Ralph Edwards called my mom a few weeks after she heard the news to ask for her help in his *This Is Your Life* tribute to my father, she had readily agreed. My father was the love of my mother's life. She always was and always remained his greatest advocate. So she agreed to help Edwards, and even appeared on the show herself.

My mother loathed being in front of a camera, and she hated the sound of her own voice. Yet she sat there next to the man who had been her husband of twenty-three years, and when Edwards quizzed her about who was the better cook, she replied, "Well we each have our specialties, so together we add up to be one pretty good cook." Then, when Edwards brought me and my brother and sister-in-law out to hug my dad, she said, "We're all very proud to be Vincent Price's family." I still can hardly bear to watch that video of her trying not to let anyone see her total terror of what lay ahead.

A week later, on the day before Thanksgiving, my mother sat me down to tell me that she and my father would no longer be married. I don't remember feeling anything when she told me. But I do remember exactly what I said to her. I reached over and held her hand and said, "Don't worry, Mom. We'll be fine. He's never home anyway. It won't be that different." In my simplistic childhood logic, I figured everything would be the same as it had always been—we'd just see less of my dad than we already did. I knew that from then on my job was to make sure that my mother would be okay. The effect my dad's departure would have on my own life was something I never let myself feel.

In the summer between sixth and seventh grade, my mother moved us from our Beverly Hills mansion to a small apartment on the other side of Los Angeles County. I went from attending the same school with the same kids for the past nine years and having unconventional, often absent, but otherwise traditionally married parents—to being the new kid in school, living with a woman having a nervous breakdown who was so ashamed of her divorce that she asked me never to tell anyone who my father was. She was terrified and sick, her fear so palpable that it filled the dark and depressing rooms of our shag-carpeted popcorn-ceilinged new apartment. Yet I never saw her cry. Every day she got out of bed and "got on with it," determined to do whatever it took to get over the loss of the person who had been her love, her husband, her partner, and her teammate.

I was eleven years old when I entered seventh grade that fall. Although I had always been the youngest girl in my class, I had never felt much different than the other kids. Now the other girls felt practically like grownups. I didn't enter puberty until I was almost fifteen, so all through junior high, when I was surrounded by weepy emotional girls who seemed to cry at the drop of a hat, I had no idea what all the hormonal fuss was about.

In fact, as time wore on, I came to be regarded as the weirdo who never cried. Everyone noticed. It became a thing. We were a particularly close class, even more so after we all spent three weeks in the spring of 1976 piled into the back of five station wagons traveling from Boston to Virginia on a Bicentennial Tour. Months before our ninth-grade graduation, everyone started talking about how sad it was going to be to have to say goodbye to one another. Even the boys agreed. For me, it just felt like another door was closing, so I needed to plan for the next one opening: high school.

Those girls weren't about to let me off the hook. "Of course you'll cry at graduation," they told me. Soon they had started a betting pool about whether or not I would shed tears in June. I could have told them not to waste their money. I couldn't even imagine what would make them *want* to cry. Of course, I never shed a tear. Not when I graduated from ninth grade, not when my mother sent me to Germany on my own for thirteen months, not when I left for college, not when I found myself temporarily paralyzed with whiplash after a car accident during my sophomore year, not when I got dumped for the first time.

I saw my heart of stone as the rock that got me through everything that had ever felt too hard to handle.

19

FALSE EVIDENCE
APPEARING REAL

My parents lived very, very busy lives. Too busy to have a child, really. Too busy often to feel their own emotions, let alone those of their little girl. Not only was I taught not to feel, but I was also taught to solve my problems on my own. I spent much of my childhood alone. My mother and father were often away from home, or they sent me away to summer camps, trips with friends, a year abroad, school programs overseas. I led the privileged life of essentially an only child, who found safety in the pages of my books and the stories I made up in my mind instead of in people.

As a little girl I was sent down to the beach to play for six hours at a stretch by myself. I was always encouraged to write stories, draw, and read up in my room. My parents exhorted me to learn to enjoy my own company. I still do. For that I will always be grateful. But fear and loneliness always kept tugging at my shirttails—just as they had my mother.

From the time I was seven years old, we lived with an armed security guard in our home. Shortly after the Manson murders, we arrived at our beach house one evening to find all the furniture slashed and everything covered with "blood" (which turned out to be catsup). My mother's anxiety spiraled out of control, and the security guard arrived shortly thereafter. My mother's fear for me filled my life like an eerie presence.

⌒

"You must be lonely," fear said over breakfast at Vacation Village, when I was seven. In an effort to have some much-needed private time, my parents sent me to the hotel dining room with a newspaper to read along with instructions on how to leave the proper tip. They told me this was good practice for becoming a grownup, and that I should observe everyone around me so I could tell them about anything interesting I'd seen or heard. To this day, I love eating at restaurants alone and making up stories about all my fellow diners. At the time, however, I just wished I could be with my parents or with my friends. I spent enough time alone at home—I didn't need more on vacation.

"I bet you wish you could go home," fear needled the summer I was twelve on the airplane to summer camp in Colorado. This was my second year at that same camp, and I didn't have very many good memories of my previous summer there. Before I'd left for camp that first year, my mother, my dad, and I had been living as a family together in our big house in Beverly Hills. I came back to a newly divorced mother who was barely holding it together in an apartment on the far reaches of the San Fernando Valley. As it turned out, my second summer in Colorado was one of the best summers of my life—but even now, I often feel that old, anxious ache in my heart whenever I leave home.

"You could die and no one would find you," fear clamored, when a man I had just met took me on a midnight "tour" of Hamburg's red light district, the infamous Reeperbahn, the year my mother banished me to a school in Germany when I turned sixteen, ostensibly due to my grades (though actually prompted by her own fear of my leaving her behind for my friends). The terror I felt for the first few months living in a foreign country whose language I couldn't speak felt immense. Eventually, however, I grew to love living in Germany. I adored my host family and all my new friends. It proved to be what still remains the best year of my entire life.

As a little girl, my response to feeling fear was taking more and more risks. I rode horses with names like Nip n Tuck who gleefully tossed me over fences. I took pride in being sent to the principal's office for any offense. Whatever misadventures I had, they were badges of honor: I was not going to end up afraid like my mother.

As I grew up, however, fear began to succeed in getting my attention. Like a car salesman who won't stop until you've bought the car you never really wanted with all of the bells and whistles you absolutely don't need, fear's whole livelihood depends on us buying into it. All of us do, though none of us really want to admit it. It's only by facing down our fears that we begin to recognize fear as the liar it always is. Gradually, we come to know that fear is really just False Evidence Appearing Real.

⁓

To fully heal fear and come back home to our hearts, we have to disempower it by understanding it was never ours. I had no intention of letting my mother's fears become my own. The moment I did, I gave them a foothold in me. The fears of our forebears often find homes in us long before we become aware of their presence.

Like my mother, I have also been ashamed to be afraid. I see myself as a strong woman who has made her way through the world essentially alone my whole life. What I couldn't see until I began my daily practice of joy were all the ways that fear clamped down over my heart.

First, I had to recognize that the legacy of fear my mother seemed to have passed down to me had been passed down to her, too. Recognizing that, I was able to stop blaming her by seeing that she had been just like me.

As we get older, we either expand into love or contract into fear. Expansion equals joy, curiosity, and openness of mind, heart, and spirit. Contraction equals doubt, rigidity, judgment, closed-mindedness, and ultimately a shut-down heart.

The older my mother got, the more fearful she became. She looked in the mirror and saw everything she did not like about herself. She looked at her daughter and was afraid that my unruly approach to life would doom me.

The older my dad got, the freer he became. The less he cared about what other people thought, and the more joyful his life grew.

When I began my daily practice of joy, I chose to live with my dad's expansive wide-open heart. But a lifetime of fear left very little room for me to really let Love in. I hadn't grasped how much I had allowed my mother's messages of fear to seep into my psyche: fear of what others would think. Fear of losing the approval of others. Even fear for my own safety. For decades, I had been living with my own armed security guard . . . in my head.

20

THE TRUTH THAT DARES TO SPEAK ITS NAME IS LOVE

When I came out to my mother during my first Christmas vacation after college graduation in 1984 at age 22, I hoped that the new love that had cracked open my heart would help me say goodbye once and for all to the fear that had shut down my emotions for so long.

Toward the end of my visit to her opulent pre–Civil War brownstone on the sunny side of Commonwealth Avenue in Boston, I found the courage to tell her that I had fallen in love with a woman. What I didn't tell her was that my girlfriend had dumped me for one of my closest friends, and that I was devastated. I never got the chance because we never got that far in the conversation. My mother's face turned steely, as I had often seen it do growing up. We sat there in uncomfortable silence, until I left for dinner with friends.

When I returned three hours later, she was sitting where I had left her. I stood awkwardly in the doorway to her living room. She told me that she had been crying and that I had broken her heart. I had never, ever seen her cry.

She told me never to tell my father, because this would break his heart, too. I honestly can't remember what else she said. The whole rest of my visit is a blur. But I do know that when I left a day later, neither of us thought that we wouldn't see one another again for three years. Yet that's what happened.

It felt like I was walking away from a complex symbiotic, enmeshed relationship that I never imagined could or would end.

Getting on my flight the next morning, looking out the window at a foggy East Coast sky, I remembered that I hadn't called my mother from the airport to say goodbye, something I had always done. I felt both free and heartbroken. Whatever else my mother had or hadn't been in my life, she had always been there.

I dropped out of acting grad school three weeks later and wound up living in the mountains of New Mexico for the next three dark difficult years, during which time my mother refused to entertain another conversation about my personal life. After the first of those three years, I suggested that perhaps I could come visit her and we could talk things through together. She said, "I refuse to talk about this. If that's what you want to do when you are here, then don't come at all." I didn't.

We didn't speak for another two years, not until 1987, when my father called and asked me to have lunch with my mother— telling me that he didn't want her to leave all of the money he sent her every month to anyone but me. We both knew that wasn't the real reason he had called; it was clear her fundamental beliefs about inheritance would never change. I knew he was asking me because he wanted us all to heal. By that time, I had come out to my dad—and not only had I not broken his heart, but we had become closer than ever. He wanted the same for my mother and for me.

A few months later, my mom and I met in New York City for lunch together at the restaurant of her choosing which happened to be in the newly built Trump Tower. We sat in the open cafe in the middle of an immense 1980s opulent marble-and-gold lobby—about the least intimate location imaginable—and made uncomfortable small talk. As I was eating my salad, she looked at me and said, "I had forgotten how quickly you ate." It was the only time she ever acknowledged that we had not spoken for three years.

We made a kind of peace over the remaining fifteen years of her life. I came to think of our relationship as a football field—large but with clear boundaries that neither of us ever crossed. (Politics were off limits, for example.) Nonetheless, despite her ongoing steely silence, I continued to talk about my life with my partner. No matter what I told her, she never responded. So I just kept shouting into the wind of her silence.

At the end of her life, many of my mother's friends asked her why she couldn't just accept my partner and be happy for me. They told me that her answer was always the same: "I'm afraid of what will happen to me if I condone her sinful lifestyle."

Afraid? That she would go to hell? Her church didn't believe in hell. But still, somehow she believed that if she accepted me, God would condemn her. The irony was that she had countless gay friends. Her most important mentors throughout her career had been gay men. Toward the end of her life, she herself mentored a number of gay men embarking on careers in design and historic preservation. Who *they* loved wasn't problematic. It was just me. It was that what I did with my life reflected on her. Just as my childhood ebullience had brought on the fear that she would be seen as the permissive mother of a Beverly Hills Brat, the fact that her daughter was a lesbian created a deep spiritual anxiety in her that she would be judged for my "sins." It was a fundamental and crippling anxiety she never found a way to heal.

The real irony was that I was wrestling as much as she was with my being a lesbian—just for different reasons. I had struggled from the moment I fell in love with a woman during my last semester of college. Up until then, I had had boyfriends, but I was also drawn to women, which both excited and scared me. Still, except for being kissed by a woman I intellectually admired but to whom I was not the least bit attracted, the whole idea of being in a relationship with a woman remained entirely in my head. Actually, to be honest, pretty much everything I did in college remained in my head. Which is to say I spent a lot of time wondering what it all meant—including being attracted to both men and women.

Falling in love with my roommate's best friend Isabel came as a total shock. Not just because she was a woman, but because I made it to almost 22 without ever having fallen in love at all. Overnight, I found myself totally and completely outside of any and every comfort zone I had ever known. I had hopped a bullet train that not only had no stops, but also had no seats, windows, or walls—just an open platform hurtling at Mach speed to who knew where.

Love. It does that. I just didn't know that then. All I wanted was a strap, a seat belt, some kind of familiar sense of safety—and I wanted it from the person with whom I was in love. I had no clue that that wasn't her job description. Lover, partner, safety net. I figured it was a package deal. I had no idea that falling in love doesn't come with a lifetime guarantee against pain and suffering and 24-hour tech support for our souls. I thought something was wrong with me for feeling so anxious and insecure, vulnerable and needy at the same time. And I was too embarrassed to ask for help.

The upshot of all of this was that what could have been such a beautiful time in my life wasn't. There I was, in love for the first time. Miserable and over the moon. I couldn't stop dancing, but I stumbled over every elating and excruciating step.

I tried forcing myself back out onto the *terra firma* of my familiar landmarks of public bravado and external self-confidence. But my trying to "act as if"—as if I was totally cool with this whole new in-love me—wasn't made any easier by the fact that this was 1984, and the person I was in love with was the same gender as me.

Two years earlier, I had spent the summer of 1982 living in Soho with my gay guy friends who were talking about an unknown "gay disease." Two years later, AIDS was killing people I knew. Gay people were scared, while straight people were either pretending AIDS didn't exist or claiming it as divine retribution for sexual sins. It was *not* a fun time to come out. Actually, it was scary as shit! Sure, to a few people, being in a relationship with a woman made me cool and even more unconventional than I already was. I was thought of as an artsy iconoclast, an image I liked to cultivate. But artsy was one thing. Gay was another.

I had grown up in Hollywood. We lived across the street from Rock Hudson. My "gay uncles" Rupert and Frank—one Grace Kelly's publicist, the other an Oscar-winning producer—were among my parents' closest friends. Everyone knew Rock, Rupert, and Frank were gay, but because they were successful and famous, no one talked about it.

I knew that to love a woman and to want to be an actress meant a life of hiding—a life I already knew too well. After having hidden the identity of my father from anyone new for more than a decade to assuage my mother's shame, I didn't want to hide anything anymore. My mother had even asked me to lie to my father about what kind of car she drove so she wouldn't be judged for how she spent her alimony. Hiding had become a habit that was hard for me to break, and I didn't like it.

When I fell in love for the first time, I chose not to lie. That's why I came out. But something niggled at me. I still felt wildly uncomfortable in my own skin. At first I thought it was because although I loved women, I never felt comfortable identifying as a lesbian. I used to joke that the word "lesbian" sounded more like a disease than anything signifying love. But that was just me deflecting my own discomfort. The fact of the matter was that I never felt like the women I knew who identified as lesbians. My friends told me I was homophobic. I was pretty sure I wasn't. Still I wore that hairshirt for a while. It scratched the hell out of me, but it never really fit.

Nonetheless *something* didn't feel right—a feeling that persisted for another three decades. At the time, however, I attributed my discomfort around my sexuality to what had happened with my mother.

She had always told me that she thought of me as her best friend. I wanted to believe her, but when I needed her most, her fear of God's condemnation proved greater than her love for me. I had hoped that love would crack open my heart, but the person whose love I wanted most saw me as a sinner. She could never fully open her heart to me so I never fully opened my own heart to anyone else.

The years that followed—my early twenties—were the hardest years of my life. Literally. A few years after coming out to my mom, I began experiencing a profoundly disturbing physical sensation: I felt something in my heart, something physically hard. It seemed to get harder and harder.

Until one afternoon, I was listening to a Joni Mitchell album in my car and suddenly tears filled my eyes and my chest welled up in pain. For the first time in twenty years, I began to cry!

As Joni sang about the crocuses she would bring to school tomorrow, tears came pouring out of me—and with them an almost unbearable ache in my heart for my dad and the sweet memory of my elementary school days when he sent little pots of crocuses with me to put on our classroom window sill so my friends and I could watch them grow. I realized how much I had been missing my dad—ever since my parents' divorce. The tears that had been hidden away for so long that I had forgotten they were even there finally flowed, foreign and unfamiliar in all their tender sorrow.

I remember watching myself cry as though I were in a movie of my own life, thinking, as I wept with both discomfort and relief, *Ahhh. So* this *is why people cry*.

As my tears fell, that stony place in my heart began to release. Over time, I gradually became "normal"—someone who cries at movies, sappy commercials, relationships ending. Yet my mother's voice continued to remonstrate me for feeling sorry for myself.

Then I discovered the actual meaning of the word "sin." Rather than some edict from on high, it is an archery term meaning to miss the mark. Realizing that, everything shifted. The only mark we can miss is to choose fear instead of acting from Love. Whenever my mother acted from fear, she missed the mark of Love. When I followed in her footsteps, so did I. Neither of us could fully open our hearts because both of us were afraid we were sinners. All either of us had ever needed to do to save our souls was to crack our hearts open to Love. I began to learn how to open myself up to tears despite her childhood teachings to the contrary, but some of her other thorny life lessons were more difficult to extricate.

We can never truly love until we learn how to forgive. But we can never truly forgive until we learn how to love. Now, thirty years later, I cry often and deeply—but it wasn't until I learned to forgive that I began not only to weep tears of joy but also to find joy in my tears—the tears that finally washed us both clean.

In order to fully step into my daily practice of joy, I knew I had to finally release myself from her sentence of sin. That meant I had to release her too. I needed to embark on a journey of forgiveness.

PART FIVE

CAUSING MY ANGELS TO SING

*He who cannot forgive others
breaks the bridge over
which he himself must pass.*
—Confucius

21

TELL ME, WHAT DO YOU HAVE IN THE HOUSE?

My mother died a few weeks after her 85th birthday, on March 2, 2002.

She asked me not to visit her as she grew ill. She told me that the memory she wanted me to have was of the last day we had spent together the April before. As I always did each spring, I had flown over to visit her in her home in Honolulu, where she spent half of each year. That day, we had gone on a glorious excursion—visiting hibiscus and orchid nurseries all across Oahu, driving along the coast and stopping to watch the waves roll in, having a delicious seafood lunch at a roadside stand, enjoying everything we loved best about Hawaii and one another.

Many of my friends criticized me for not overriding my mother's wishes. They wondered how I could not want to say goodbye in person. I said then what I still believe now: It was *her* death. She was allowed to choose the way she wanted to negotiate it. To my mother, appearance was everything. She asked me to see her as she had been, not as she was now. I needed to honor that in her dying, as I always had in her living. I was not about to change when she needed to count on me most.

By mid-February, my mother no longer knew who I was when I called her on the phone, as I did every day.

She had asked me not to tell anyone she was ill. Only a handful of people knew. Once I realized she was getting close to transitioning, however, I reached out to a few additional good friends of hers so that her death would not come as a total shock to them.

On the evening of March 1, my mother and I spoke on the phone. For the previous weeks, the nurses had simply held the phone up to her ear so I could tell her I loved her. But that night, my mother came back. She asked me how I was, what was happening in my life, and she told me how often she thought of me and how much she loved me. I told her that the trees had started blooming early that year. They were already popping up pink and white. The crocuses were out. Soon the daffodils would follow. Spring was coming, I told her. I felt it in the air. Then, as always, I told her how much I loved her. When we hung up, I was filled with joy to have my mother back.

That night before I went to sleep, suddenly I panicked. My mother had asked me not to tell anyone about her illness. She was the most private person I have ever known. Would she ever be able to forgive me for betraying her confidence?

At 6 AM the next morning, the phone rang. The nurses told me that my mother had passed.

I walked through the next few days in a haze. I had known it was coming, of course. I was incredibly grateful to have had the opportunity to say goodbye. Yet her passing hit me hard. I had already experienced the deaths of both my stepmother and my beloved father almost a decade earlier. Why did this feel so different?

My 40th birthday was just a month away—so it seemed like a silly word to use for an adult—but I realized I felt like an orphan. I felt alone in the world in a way I never had before.

~

A week or so after my mother's passing, I received a call from a woman named Laura who told me that she was repairing some of my mother's Navajo textiles. She had tracked me down to ask me to come by her studio so we could discuss what to do with them.

We arranged to meet a few days later, after a lunch I had scheduled with my partner and one of my closest friends. As it all turned out, the three of us so enjoyed our lunch together that I asked them to come with me.

We climbed up a narrow flight of stairs and knocked at the door. A smiling woman a decade or so older than me invited us all in to her sunny second-story studio filled with wools and textiles. As a lifelong lover of Navajo weaving, I was in seventh heaven. I oohed and aahed as she gave us the tour before we all sat down to chat.

"I never met your mother," Laura began. "But we talked a lot on the phone. I felt like I got to know her quite well through our conversations. When I read in the paper that she died, I felt concerned because I didn't know what to do with these textiles. I have six of them, and they're valuable. I didn't have any other contact information. So I decided to ask your mother what to do. Then I waited to hear from her."

I tried to keep my focus on Laura and not look at my partner and my friend, but I couldn't help wondering if they were thinking what I was thinking. Was this woman cracked? She seemed perfectly normal, but . . .

"The next morning your mother came into my studio, over there," Laura continued, nodding to her left at the second-story window. I nodded back, trying to keep my gaze steady and non-committal. "Now, I had no idea what your mother looked like, but I just knew this was her. So I asked her what she wanted me to do. She told me, 'Be consistent with our agreement.'

"Well, that was exactly what she would have said," Laura went on, "and so I continued to restore the pieces. I just wanted to let you know."

"Yes," I heard myself saying. "That *is* just what my mother would have said." Not quite believing my own words.

Laura smiled at me, a little relieved, I think, that I had affirmed her experience. So she risked one more observation: "You know, I've come to believe that when people die, they stick around for a week or two before leaving, just to make sure that they've taken care of business. And then they go."

Again I felt myself nodding.

"But eventually they come back," Laura added. "After about a year, they come back for good, and they're with you forever."

I stared at her, not knowing what to say. So I opted for polite and terse. "Ah, yes," I responded. "That all sounds good. Thank you so much for telling me. I'll let the executor of my mom's estate know that's what you're doing."

I couldn't get out of there fast enough. When we got to the bottom of the stairs, I turned to my companions and blurted out, "Do you think it's true?"

"You mean that your mother came to her through the window?" my partner asked. I knew my partner believed in ghosts, having experienced some amazing paranormal encounters herself.

"No. No. That sounded exactly like my mom. Not that. Do you think it's true that she'll come back and be with me for the rest of my life?" I asked, genuinely horrified at the thought.

They both smiled reassuringly at me.

"Oh, no," my friend said. "I'm sure that won't happen."

I wanted to believe them. I needed to feel that I was finally free of hearing my mother's voice telling me what to do and who to be.

In the days that followed my mother's death, as my sorrow had begun to lift, I had realized something profound. Although I missed her presence, I would not miss her big opinion about every aspect of my life. Although my mother and I had found our peace in the years after we reconciled, she never was able to resist telling me what she felt was the best way to do or be or say anything. Whenever I came to visit her, she always asked me what I was bringing in the way of clothes—and then proceeded to verbally repack my suitcase so it would meet her fashion expectations.

There was no matter in which my mother did not feel I needed her "advice." Until the very end, my mother's One Right Way filtered into every area of my life. So when Laura told me that my mother would come back after a year, I was not even remotely pleased.

However, a year later (almost to the day), my mother did come back. I was walking on the ridge in the mountains behind my house, thinking about my horses. I found myself wishing I could talk to my mom. Despite the myriad ups and downs of our relationship, we had always found our common ground talking about animals—my horses or dogs, even the Iditarod or dolphins. Anything to do with animals was a safe and joy-filled topic.

I heard myself saying out loud, "What should I do, Mom?" Clear as a bell, I heard her answer. It was verbatim what she would have said. From that moment on, my mom was back in my life, and for the most part, in the loveliest ways: the best of my mom—her clever observations and sage pieces of advice, in witty turns of phrase and old stories I had always loved.

Until I lost everything.

⌒

In 2006, I experienced what I've come to refer to as "the perfect financial storm." Through a lethal cocktail of poor decisions, both business and personal, I lost my home, my life savings, and most of my material possessions, ending up in massive debt. In other words, about three years before the rest of this country and the world had their economic meltdown, I had mine.

At first, I was in shock. I couldn't believe this was happening. I kept thinking this was some kind of bad dream and I would just wake up. I wanted to bury my head in the sand, run away and hide, wish everything back to "normal." But literally every single day for quite a while, my situation just seemed to get worse and worse.

When I was a kid, my dad told me that when he was a freshman at Yale in 1929, the stock market crashed. A couple of his schoolmates' fathers were among the men who jumped to their deaths from the windows high above Wall Street. As a little girl, I couldn't fathom why money would make anyone want to take his own life. As an adult, I totally got it. I was flooded with shame, terror, guilt, and fear.

The moment things had fallen apart, I had begun bludgeoning myself with my mother's imagined anger and disappointment, along with daily nasty "I told you so's" and "How could you's" thrown in for good measure.

Then one day, I heard her ask me a question that held no rancor. She simply asked, "Tell me, what do you have in the house?"

I knew where that came from—a Bible story my mom loved about a woman whose husband had died, leaving her in so much debt that she felt her only solution was to sell her two sons into slavery and then kill herself. A prophet came by her house and, recognizing her distress, asked her: "Tell me, what do you have in the house?" She told him she had a little bit of oil, that's all.

He told her to go to her neighbors, borrow every vessel she could, come home, close the doors, and fill them all with the oil she had. The oil filled every vessel. Then he told her to sell it and pay off her debt.

Whenever my mother had a financial problem, she had always asked herself what she had in the house. Her answers ranged from overlooked possessions she was able to sell, to resources among friends and in her community. It was a reminder that she often already had exactly what she needed to solve her problem.

When I heard her voice asking me the same question, I remembered that I had an entire storage unit filled with boxes of my parents' things that I had not yet dealt with. Not important items—all of those had already been sold or donated to museums or archives. This was just random stuff I needed to sort through before throwing the rest out. The first thing I found was a battered leather wallet that had belonged to my dad in the 1970s. It had the name Vincent rather crudely embossed on it.

"EBay," I heard myself say. "Try eBay." I did. It worked!

Suddenly the possessions that had felt like unwanted baggage were bailing me out. Not only that, but as I sold these things, I discovered a worldwide community of my family's fans, and that led to more income from public speaking and writing articles, all while giving the fans a connection to my family that they had long been craving. It was a gift for us all.

But that didn't solve all my problems—not by a long shot. I was able to pay my own bills for a while, but I had a business that was teetering on failure. As persistent in death as she was in life, my mother kept asking me the same question: "Tell me, what do you have in the house?" Gratitude was my mother's magic word. Whenever she was fearful or overwhelmed or anxious, she counted her blessings—an inventory of her whole life always at her fingertips.

Sure enough, other solutions began to present themselves. My in-house interior designer decided to move on in his career. The thought came: "You know, you could do this yourself."

This proved to be one of the most delightful ironies of my life: My mother had been a very successful costume and architectural designer, and I had apprenticed with her growing up—working on many of her projects. Even then, I knew that the *last* thing I ever wanted to do was to follow in her footsteps. I wanted to be like my joy-filled loving dad, not my strict disciplinarian mom. Yet suddenly the design skills I had so reluctantly learned from her were a resource, and within three weeks of hanging out my shingle as a designer, I had thirteen clients!

As my new career took off, I began to earn enough money to pay off more debt. But that wasn't the greatest gift of becoming a designer. The real blessing was finding out that I was very good at something in which I had absolutely no ego investment—and then experiencing the unbelievable sense of freedom that brought.

With each new design job, I witnessed myself in wonder excelling at something with such ease—in a way I had never been able to succeed at the things I cared about most. I had so *not* wanted to become a designer that the profession—one which the world finds glamorous and creative—held no particular appeal for me. I stepped into it out of necessity. I continued it out of gratitude.

My goal was never to become famous or to develop a signature style or stamp my "look" on all my clients' homes. Without the ego attachment of my small self, I was able to show up to my own creativity in ways I had never been able to do with writing or with art.

I came into my clients' lives, listened to their stories, and used the aesthetic and resourcing skills I had learned from my mother to co-create visual spaces that reflected their truest selves back to them. Design may not have been the career I had dreamed of for myself, but it gave me the opportunity to fulfill other people's dreams instead. I absolutely adored that!

More than that, however, becoming a designer showed me what it felt like to live a life not aimed at earning the world's approval in order to "succeed." Against all odds, designing helped pave the way home to my truest self.

When in my new career I doubted my abilities, however, asking myself *What do you have in the house?* became my daily mantra. Soon it seemed like every time I needed an answer, one came. When I worried about my lack of experience in design, I found answers in areas at which I did have expertise and then applied them to my projects. In one very large room that seemed to have no focal point—just a mishmash of expensive oversized furniture all thrown together—I remembered the technique of a French painter named Eugene Boudin. Boudin used dabs of the color red to lead the viewer's eye from foreground through middle ground to the horizon. I tried that with my design, and the whole room came together beautifully. What I had in my house helped me create beautiful spaces in other people's houses.

Things were finally looking up.

Then the economy tanked. But even though my business—like everyone else's—took a huge hit, I wasn't blindsided. I went back to the Bible story. The first thing the woman did was take an inventory. Had I really done that? Sort of . . . but I had tried to ignore the effect of a lifetime of hearing family stories, which had engendered this massive fear of money in me.

When I had written about my dad's financial fears in his biography, I had viewed them objectively—as his. I hadn't yet understood how his fears had lived forward in my own life, how they had been affecting every decision I made. So some of what I had in my house demanded cleaning up and throwing out.

This was the beginning of my realization that we unconsciously live with our own stories, becoming deaf, dumb, and blind to the ways they affect every decision we make. Those stories, the litany of lies spewed by our false selves, begin to cover up all the good in our lives. We lose sight of our own resources and begin to live with our failings like a bad limp that everyone else notices except us.

I began to clean house, learning to face down my own lifelong financial fears, doubts, and habits, by asking: Tell me, what do you have in the house?

Of course, I knew that I appeared to have things that other people might not have—a famous father, a successful mother, a good education, even a storage unit full of stuff to sell on eBay. But I didn't see it that way.

Every single time I have asked myself what I have in the house, my first thought has always been *nothing*.

I thought I was paying money I didn't have for a storage unit full of boxes with who-knew-what in them. Yet the random "stuff" I found in those boxes became the oil that has filled years' worth of vessels in supplying my life in times of need.

For the life of me I didn't think that anything my mother taught me would be of use in my life. It was a lot easier to reject her teachings out of hand than to feel that I had constantly failed her expectations of me. Yet everything she had dedicated herself to teaching me—aesthetic appreciation, design skills, daily prayer, and dedicated discipline to any task at hand—these had proved my lifeline when I needed saving.

It was during this time that I learned one of the fundamental tenets of the Way of Being Lost: When you cannot turn back, you have to discover resources you never knew you had.

I couldn't wish the money back into my bank account, my house back into my comforting financial portfolio, or the shame

I felt back into hiding. Instead, I had to find the courage and the humility to turn the autopilot of my life off and look long and hard—at the stories I'd been playing out, the skills I'd forgotten I had, the useless baggage I needed to discard, and the resources that had always surrounded me. I learned, in a way I never would have otherwise, that every crisis can become an opportunity to change ourselves and the world in which we live by using everything we already are from the inside out!

⸺

Apparently, in 2012 the Universe thought it was time for me to share this latest life lesson learned. I was invited to give a TEDx talk, which I called "Tell Me, What Do You Have in the House?" As I prepared my speech, I realized how scared I was to reveal the single most shameful thing that had ever happened to me—my financial meltdown. Yet I was determined to stand up not only to the crippling guilt and shame with which I'd been living like a persistent and chronic disease, but also to my mother's voice in my head always telling me to be quiet.

When I finished my talk, all I heard were cheers; all I felt was love. The response that followed was amazing. Turns out that while I was feeling completely alone in my story, so many other people who had lost everything during the Great Recession that began in 2007 were feeling the same thing. A whole swath of America had lost just as much as I had.

My willingness to tell my story helped others share theirs with me. That showed me just how much we all isolate in our stories, living with the leprosy of loss, imagining the judgment of others. I recognized that we are all struggling to shed the shadow of shame and reconnect with the joy and hope and supply that are our birthright. When one of us has the courage to share our truth—however shameful it may feel—we all feel less alone. By speaking in the voice of my truest self, I saw that I could help others find their own ways to heal their old stories too.

By having the courage to defy my mother's edict about not talking too much about all the wrong things to all the wrong people, I also realized something else that shook me to my core. As I crafted my TEDx talk, I gained a new perspective on my mother. While I had been beating myself up with all the ways I imagined her hating me for what I had allowed to happen, she had actually been there trying to help. By asking me what I had in the house, she was reminding me of all the resources she knew I had—including, perhaps especially, her love for me.

That both comforted and confused me. How could my mother's voice in my head make me feel so terrible about myself at the same time as it was giving me the help I needed? Which mother was the real one? The mother who verbally beat me up or the mother who wanted to help me? I knew which one I wanted it to be, but I couldn't stop hearing the one who berated me with my failure. I had to find a way to stop this vicious cycle.

On this road trip we call life, we all need fellow travelers and companions on our journey. It is no coincidence that the person who helped me heal my oldest mother wounds was a woman whose name is also Mary.

22

TAKING MY MOTHER TO CHINA

I met Mary in 2008, when she walked into my gallery for reasons that she still can't quite explain—even to herself. Her husband had passed away earlier that year, and she had spent six months just sitting, reading, feeling his absence, dipping her toes in the murky and unfamiliar waters of life without him. But one day the thought came to her to drive over and ask for my help getting her home ready for a design tour.

I've never believed that we meet people by chance, but rather I believe that everyone comes into our lives for a reason. Although I was usually out of the gallery with clients or on job sites, I was there when Mary stopped by to arrange a consultation. Of course, I had an unusual opening in my schedule the next afternoon.

Thus began our creative collaboration. From what could have been merely a month of fabric shopping and furniture rearranging, we have built a deep, lasting, extraordinary friendship!

Three weeks after I met Mary, we were walking down the street when suddenly I saw the two of us as though I were filming the scene from a distance. Our smiling faces and our genuine enjoyment of one another's company. In that instant, I understood that I was there to help illuminate the next steps on Mary's path out of grief and back to joy. This thought came next: *What I am doing with this Mary is exactly what I used to do with my mother Mary—but this Mary sees me for who I am, not who she wanted me to be.* That's when I knew that Mary would help me jettison some of the very deep mother baggage I had been lugging around for decades.

That said, it was months before Mary would even agree to go to lunch with me. Like me, she guards her time, her heart, and her trust. But slowly, very slowly, we let one another in as we began to talk about the many mutual passions we shared— poetry, literature, art, design, cars, travel, prayer, adventure, and God.

It wasn't long before I realized that I had found an extraordinary new friend who just happened to be thirty years my senior. I think most people thought that Mary was a kind of mother figure to me. I firmly resisted that appellation because to me, calling someone a "mother figure" was damning them with very faint praise indeed.

I said to myself: *Mary is nothing like my mother. She never expects a thing of me, never judges me for my actions or friendships, never exaggerates my failings, and never condemns my dark places.* My mother had been terrified of my big free spirit and tried to rein it in with "common sense," but whenever I told Mary I wanted to jump, she'd grin and ask, "How high?"

In so many other ways, however, she did remind me very much of my mother—with her high standards, innate elegance, steely backbone, and definite opinions. But instead of seeing this Mary through a fractured glass of expectations, I was given the gift of seeing and being seen through the reflective lens of Love.

Mary's life motto is "Oh what fun!" She lives it—no holds barred, no exceptions to the rule. If, as we get older, we either expand into our lives or contract into our fears, Mary has gone beyond expanding. She has exploded. Every day, Mary has shown me all the ways I want to age—with curiosity, an open heart, irreverence, joy, humor, and love. Because of Mary, I began to crawl my way out of some very dark places that had threatened to take away my joy for good: the shame and secrecy and silence that came with being my mother's daughter. With Mary I could talk about anything.

Mary also became the role model I needed when I decided to change my life after that moment in the mirror. Very early on in our friendship, she had told me the story of knowing that she needed to go back to school in her late forties to become a nurse practitioner, and that the only school she wanted to go to was Harvard. Because her youngest child was still in high school, her decision raised eyebrows. She stuck to her guns, knowing—just as she had known as a 19-year-old that she could not pursue her parents' dream of her becoming a teacher but instead needed to become a nurse—that she had to listen to her own truth and live it. She did indeed go to Harvard and became a nurse practitioner. At a time when I was trying to find the courage to live my own dreams, Mary's story became a lifeline.

Poet Galway Kinnell tells us that "everything flowers from within, of self-blessing; though sometimes it is necessary to reteach a thing its loveliness, to put a hand on the brow of the flower, and retell it in words and in touch it is lovely, until it flowers again from within, of self-blessing."

Whenever I experienced dark nights of the soul, I would think of how Mary saw me—always in my highest light, always as my best self, always in pure love. I thought about her high standards, her inability to suffer fools, her deep-rooted pragmatism, and I thought, *If Mary sees me as being worthy of love, as being capable of doing all the things I am afraid I will never do or be, then it must be true. So I am going to act as if I am the me that Mary sees.* Mary retaught me my own loveliness. What more can any of us do for one another but to retell one another that we are lovely, until we flower again from within, of self-blessing?

That's why, when out of the blue Mary told me that she wanted to send me to China, I didn't say no. It was hard not to decline, hard to believe that I deserved such an unbelievable gift. When my mother was alive, I often talked about taking her to China—where she had spent the five most important and memorable years of her childhood. The Grant family—my grandparents and their three children—lived in Shanghai for almost five years. It became one of my mother's most cherished memories. Her love of Hawaii, which became one of her homes, stemmed from the unforgettable childhood memory that she so often described to me of living in a place where she could take off her tight Western shoes and itchy stockings and feel the humid warm tropical air on her bare skin. She became a lifelong sun worshipper and lover of all things Asian.

My dear Mary knew this story, and she knew that the time was right for me to go. Together, she and I created our three-week dream trip to China. It was "our" trip in every sense of the word: a trip of three Marys—for, like my mother, my first name is also Mary. Anchored in the safety of sharing the trip virtually with my Mary waiting for me at home, this Mary (me) could take the memory of my mother Mary on the trip to China that I had been dreaming of for decades.

It would be a Journey of Forgiveness.

As I began preparing for China—making and remaking my packing lists and going over my upcoming itinerary—I began rereading *A Course in Miracles*. I thought I knew the Course pretty well, but up to that point, I had managed to miss its most crucial teaching: Forgiveness is not only the key to happiness, but it is the key to our salvation.

Salvation, according to the Course, is not some Cecil B. DeMille meets Dante Saved from the Fire and Brimstone of the Circles of Hell. It is waking up from the dream that we ever were or will be separate from God. The Course believes that every encounter we have with another person can be a holy encounter each time we see another person as no different from ourselves. As I see others, I see myself. As I treat others, I treat myself. As I think of others, I think of myself. In another, I either find or lose myself. If I want to learn that I am blessed, I must be willing to bless you.

As the trip grew closer and I began to pack my material belongings, I realized I was going to need to unpack my whole relationship with my mother—to find our holy connection and release all the ways in which our mother-daughter symbiosis still had us both stuck.

From this unpacking our relationship through the lens of forgiveness, I realized that I had stopped remembering my mother as she was and instead had transformed her into a kind of Mother Avatar who played a wide range of roles: Moral Authority, Disciplinarian, Depriver, Judge, Condemner. After my financial life fell apart, I had assigned her the Mother Avatar role so that her voice in my head could serve as a bulwark to my own fear and disappointment and doubt. In other words, I hated myself for all the ways I had failed, so I used her old familiar voice to beat me up for it. Only through forgiveness could I release us both.

From the heart of forgiveness, I began to release that avatar, and in doing so, I started to catch small glimpses of my mother as just another person, like me, trying to heal her fears. Then, in one light-bulb moment, I saw that all those things I had perceived and decried as judgment, fear, timidity, rigidity, and rules had actually just been her ways, however imperfect, of loving me! She had been trying to give me tools so that my life could be better than hers. It was when my fears slammed up against hers that I got caught up in the spin cycle of react, rebel, resent, and resist.

⌐⌐

Two weeks before I left for China, I received an envelope in the mail with a Boston postmark and no return address. On the back of the envelope was a child's sticker, large and white, with a big yellow shooting star that read, "You are brilliant. You're a star!" When I opened the envelope, there was no note inside, only a copy of my mother's death certificate. The date of her death was March 2, 2002—eleven years to the day I was to leave for China.

I have no idea who sent that missive, but its message was loud and clear.

Later that afternoon, I boarded a plane and began the journey of a lifetime.

23

MY MOTHER TONGUE

I arrived in China with the goal of understanding my mother's childhood. By experiencing the place where she had grown up, I hoped to understand how it had influenced the whole rest of her life. I thought I would see what she had seen and feel what she had felt as a little girl.

I hoped to find my mother's true self as a means of replacing what had become the bludgeoning voice of my mother in my head, which was the language in which both of our false selves spoke. But sometimes the ways I encountered my mother on the trip surprised even me.

Whenever I travel to a foreign country, I've always had a tendency to adapt my speech to my surroundings. In China, it took me a couple of days to realize that I was mimicking my guides. In every region, I had a different guide—each of whom spoke a different accented and idiomatic English. I realized that I was changing my speech patterns, almost unconsciously, so that after a few days together, I began slowing down, leaving out unnecessary words, using their idioms, and becoming monosyllabic and stilted. Frankly, it sounded both condescending and dorky.

It's human nature when we catch ourselves doing something embarrassing to try to let ourselves off the hook by blaming someone else. I once went on a horseback ride on a friend's ranch in Montana. It was the first ride of the season, so the horses were frisky, which resulted in a series of mostly funny mishaps. The wrangler's wife had decided to join us. Toward the end of our six-hour ride as we were heading back to the barn, her horse started to buck. Instead of trying to get the horse under control, she just let it buck away while she yelled at her husband, "Goddamn it, Dave. Goddamn it, Dave." Over and over again. As I watched myself mimic my guides, I Goddamn-it-Dave'd my own mother, because I suddenly realized this embarrassing linguistic idiosyncrasy had actually come from her.

My mother was an inveterate but mostly unconscious mimic. Whenever we caught a cab together, my rather proper Anglo-Saxon mother would suddenly morph into an Irishwoman, Bostonian, or East Indian, depending on the nationality or ethnic background of the driver, settling into a lively conversation in his or her native brogue, accent, or dialect. Her specialty was Pidgin, the common parlance used to communicate across cultures throughout the Pacific Rim, which she used with abandon while living in Honolulu.

Mary Grant grew up being shuffled, as she liked to say, from pillar to post in four different countries—Wales, England, China, and Canada—before immigrating to the United States by herself at the age of 18. She was born during World War I while her father was off fighting for the Scots National Guard in Gallipoli. My grandfather survived, but he came back to an almost nonexistent job market in the United Kingdom. So when he and my grandmother, who had met while they were both studying at a dairy college in Scotland, were offered a job running the dairy in Shanghai that brought pasteurization to China, they took it.

My mother was five. Because she was much younger than her older brother and sister, my mother was with an *amah* (an East Asian nanny) who taught her Pidgin while her siblings were in school. As many colonials do in a foreign country, the Grants lived much better than they had in the U.K., in a very large, white, Western-style house in the French Concession, with servants and trips to the countryside to escape the summer heat. After her father chose to relocate the family to British Columbia shortly before my mother's tenth birthday—a global move that would drive the Grants into increasing poverty during the Depression—my mother came to think of her time in Shanghai as the best of her childhood.

My mother went on to study French in high school, as well as Italian and Spanish as an adult. Whenever she traveled, she loved to speak in the native tongue of whatever country she visited. I was proud to have inherited my mother's love for and gift with languages. When I lived in Germany as a teenager studying abroad, I became so fluent in German that whenever I mentioned an experience I had had in the United States, people thought I had lived in the U.S. as an exchange student, instead of the other way around. What I hadn't wanted to see until I went to China was that I had also inherited her aptitude for mimicry.

When you mimic someone, whether consciously or not, what you're really doing is paying attention and finding common ground. That, of course, was what my mother had been doing not only on all those multicultural cab rides, but for her whole life. The girl who had been moved from pillar to post was trying to fit in.

When my St. Louis–born father met my English mother at a dinner party in Bel Air, California, he turned to her and said, "You know, I've never met anyone from the Bronx." My mother burst out laughing. When she began her career as a designer, she had worked in New York City's Fashion District, where people had poked fun at her British accent. So she had changed it. By the time she met my father, my mother sounded like a New Yorker from the Bronx. Within a few years of settling down in California after their marriage, however, Mary Grant Price sounded like she had spent her whole life on the West Coast.

At the end of her life, my mother had homes in Boston, Santa Fe, Los Angeles, and Honolulu. She adapted her speech to the dialects of each place as naturally as breathing. She couldn't even hear herself do it.

Before my mother died, I had dreamed of taking her to China so she could revisit the place where she had grown up. Well, I finally did—in a different way than I had originally envisioned. I took her love of language, her desire to see and experience many countries and cultures, her unconscious desire to eradicate the difference between herself and others through communication, her gritty self-determination not to live a provincial life, and her expansive love of the world. I took the mother I knew, and I tried to make China explain what I wanted to see about her. I cut and pasted my memory of her on top of the place where she spent her childhood and looked for easy answers that would explain her.

That, I found out, is *not* forgiveness.

Taking my mother to China on a journey of forgiveness actually meant being willing to release all of my stories of her as well as all of my stories of "me." All the Goddamn-it-Dave blaming, all the ways I wanted to be different from her, all the ways I used her voice in my head to do my dirty work.

The journey of forgiveness takes us from blame to blessing if we can see one another as we are instead of who we want one another to be. The Chinese person living on the other side of the world in a country precariously poised between capitalist boom and communist oppression is no different from me—the tall blonde Westerner—the moment we can both see that we are all simply trying to live a life of peace and meaning. I had to learn to see my mother with the same unclouded eyes of Love with which I saw a stranger on the other side of the world.

⌐⌐

At the end of her life, my mother finally told me something I had always known. We had just finished a late breakfast in a brightly lit coffee shop in Waikiki. For a woman who surrounded herself with jewel-tone opulent Victorian splendor, I always found it fascinating that she felt most at ease eating at plain Jane coffee shops. She had her favorite spots, where the servers knew her by name, gave her a Naugahyde booth with a view of the room, and always remembered that she liked both her bacon and hash browns extra crispy. She loved this one for its vintage pastel color scheme and low-key glimpse at the frenetic tourist scene on Honolulu's most famous beach. We had just finished eating when she finally shared something she must have wanted to release for decades.

From the time I was born, she told me, she saw how much my father loved me. That terrified her, she said, because she thought it would kill him if something ever happened to me. From that moment on, she had been afraid. She was 45 years old, and all of her friends' children were teenagers already. She had helped raise my brother, her stepson, but only after he became a teenager. Whenever something would happen to me as a baby—when I was fussy or flatulent, uncomfortable or restless—she felt too embarrassed to ask her friends for their advice, feeling that she should have known the answers herself. She read everything she could get her hands on, but she still could not shake the fear that something bad might happen to her baby.

That fear, something all mothers have, began to spiral out of control. What she did not know when she was talking to me as an adult that afternoon in Waikiki was that I was aware of how dependent she became during my childhood on a regime of caffeine, pills, alcohol, and antacids. She took uppers and copious amounts of coffee in the morning to carry her through a daunting routine of raising me, running a vast household, and working on films as well as on her art and design projects. Then she'd have her first martini of the day in the late afternoon, followed by a few more to take the edge off and give her the stamina and social courage for the networking and party life that she, the ultimate introvert, led with my dad. In addition, she'd take antacids to soothe what must have been a perpetual ache in her gut, the ache of abandoning herself.

That wasn't all I knew. What I knew most of all was what her fear *felt* like. I knew it because I had felt it my whole life—first as something I strongly resisted by being a child who would gleefully risk anything and later as something I hoped to shield her from. Finally, when I moved into adulthood, I felt my mother's fear in the form of my own anxieties. It was those anxieties—mounting to the point that they felt like mortal illnesses, mushrooming into myriad terrors, and eventually manifesting in panic attacks that felt like little deaths—that by my early thirties had finally shepherded me into my conscious and committed spiritual practice.

I listened to my mother's confession partly like her child and partly filled with a desire to help her in any way I could. At first, we talked about how her fear had led her to tether me to what she hoped was safety. I never once was allowed to attend a party all through high school because she was so afraid I might be exposed to alcohol or drugs.

"You should have let me make my own mistakes," I told her. "I've never been someone who liked to lose control. I didn't really ever *want* to drink or do drugs." But then I realized that she was hardly listening to me. She had one more thing she needed to say.

"I am afraid all the time," she told me.

Suddenly I stopped thinking about me, and instead I heard her from my heart. She needed me to bear witness to her.

"I am afraid of fear," she admitted.

Her calm face, her unwavering voice, her ramrod posture, her eternal composure belied what I knew to be roiling underneath.

I knew it because I, too, knew what it was to be afraid of fear.

I don't think I ever loved my mother as much as I did in that moment of her purest honesty and vulnerability.

I don't remember my response, but that conversation shifted something profound between us, leveled the playing field, made us more like peers and less like mother and daughter. From then on, we could be more honest, talk about the things that scared us.

All those years of bludgeoning ourselves with a mirage of human perfection, and at the end of my mother's life, we both finally experienced a measure of the only kind of perfect there really is: The Perfect Love that always casts out fear. Letting ourselves be vulnerable with one another *was* that Perfect Love.

I had judged my mother for letting her fear rule the day because I judged myself. I had to release that judgment by recognizing that the rules and rigidity that were such a big part of her legacy to me really just masked the terror and shame that plagued her every day. I hated her for her fear, and yet how could I, who have so often struggled with my own shame and terror, not feel compassion for her?

Many people are afraid to travel to foreign countries because they fear the differences in culture will take them too far out of their comfort zones. I love to travel and find the beautiful common ground that exists across all cultures. On my trip to China, however, I often felt fear. That perplexed me, until I finally realized it was not my own fear I was feeling. I was not afraid of spending three weeks alone halfway across the world in a country whose languages I did not speak or read. I was afraid that, like my mother, I would become so afraid of being afraid that I would never show up to my own life and do something that made a difference in the world. To face down that lie and heal, I had to forgive both her fear and my own.

My trip to China gave me the chance to fully step into Love and out of fear. As the trip progressed, I kept asking myself: Which mother will I choose to carry in my heart in the future—the one I often feared and resented for being so fearful and for imposing her fears on me, or the one for whom I have compassion?

I have never been one to travel lightly. I come with too much stuff, and I usually leave with more. China was no exception. I lugged around a too-heavy suitcase, made heavier with each gift I found to bring back. But one item in my suitcase I was determined to leave there.

When my mother died in 2002, I had hoped that the difficult parts of our relationship would die with her. In many ways they did. But there were so many old wounds that had never stopped bleeding, so many old voices, inherited from her, that had kept me from listening to my truth. As I traced those wounds, those old voices, back to my mother's fear, I knew it was up to me to heal for us both. Fear was the voice of our false selves. That voice had bludgeoned us both enough. By learning to listen to Love, I could rediscover both my mother's and my true selves.

I had taken my mother to China. It was time to leave the old baggage that no longer served either of us behind.

24

WHISTLING
MY MOTHER'S
COSTUMES

Geneva Williams was my mother's seamstress. She lived in what my mother liked to call "The Flats" of the San Fernando Valley, on a nondescript block in a nondescript beige apartment complex with a nondescript treeless front yard.

Some of the more miserable hours of my childhood were spent in the smoky haze of Mrs. Williams' cramped ecru living room, standing on a stool, being poked and prodded with pins, while my mother scrutinized every tuck and seam, every hemline and dart. I came to loathe everything about our sessions with the chain-smoking private seamstress who made our clothes. I longed to be a child whose mother took her shopping for off-the-rack outfits that made her look like the other kids. I just wanted to fit in, not to wear my mother's "creations" in which I would "look my best." But for my mother, to let me out of the house looking anything less than A-list would have been tantamount to child abuse.

In the fourth grade, a new girl named Jennifer Berger joined our class. For some reason all my girlfriends and I had an instant love-hate relationship with Jennifer. She lived in a modest neighborhood near our exclusive private school with her single mother. This alone made her unusual because in the early 1970s, the only other single mothers we knew had been tragically widowed—and this didn't seem to be the case with the attractive and competent Mrs. Berger. On top of this, Jennifer was smart, well behaved, self-possessed, and blessed with a perfect figure. At least that's how I remember her.

As we trudged through our schooldays in our shapeless grey flannel tunic uniforms with our white shirts and navy blue blazers, we could avoid the petty jealousies of having classmates with more style and panache. But on free-dress days or at birthday parties, we were all aware of Jennifer Berger's apparent perfection. I, for one, was jealous. I acted out my jealousy by wanting to wear jeans and T-shirts and cute dresses just like Jennifer's. Sadly, for the daughter of the eagle-eyed Mary Grant Price, this was not to be.

One of the phrases of my childhood that will forever be seared in my memory—a phrase that my mother persisted in using long after I changed schools, rendering Jennifer Berger a distant memory—was "No, dear. Only Jennifer Berger can wear that." This phrase was trotted out in response to almost anything I coveted that was chic, tight, trendy, or cool.

To her credit, my mother was not a thoughtless authoritarian. She firmly believed that I, like our dogs, should learn from the folly of our ways. When Puffie the pug peed on the rug, she was locked up behind the folding gate away from us—thus teaching her that if she peed in the house, she would be removed from the people she loved. Similarly, my mother believed that I should have the experience of trying on clothes that didn't look good on me so I could learn all the reasons why my high waist or long legs or wide hips made the same jeans that looked amazing on Jennifer look horrifically misguided on me.

I was a quick study. Within a few months, all I had to do was to pull something off a store rack or point it out in a magazine to elicit my mother's "only Jennifer Berger" response. Soon I came to see that the hoped-for image of myself as willowy, self-assured, trendy, and utterly perfect was not the person staring back at me from the mirror. I relinquished whatever fashion fantasy I was nurturing in favor of more body-appropriate attire as determined by my mother.

I don't mean to imply that I looked frumpy. My mother was not only of the moment, she was always ahead of her time. I was the kid dressed in next year's color scheme or fabric or silhouette. I just never looked like the me I imagined I could be if left to my own devices.

Once my mother realized that I was interested in fashion, however, she took it upon herself to teach me everything she knew—far more than I or any child not named Isaac Mizrahi or Tom Ford would ever care to learn. Soon my sessions with Mrs. Williams escalated to the point of torture: Every nip and tuck, hem and seam became an opportunity for me to learn just what did and did not look good on my body.

It took us well into my teenage years for my mother and me to reach an uneasy truce. We struck a deal: I would wear what she wanted me to wear to her events or important occasions. I could wear what I wanted to wear to my own. Most wonderful of all, the sessions with Geneva Williams mercifully came to an end. But not without having accomplished my mother's goal: I did and would forever know how to gauge what I could and could not wear.

～

Despite my unpleasant memories of my tailoring sessions with Geneva Williams, one of the things I really wanted to do in China was to have some custom blouses made. I had heard how talented and affordable the Chinese tailors were, and since most of what I can buy in stores never fits me, I was eager to see what they could do.

On my second day in Shanghai, my guide and I went to a multi-story building filled with small kiosks of tailors who sold fabric and custom-made clothing near the oldest part of the city. It took me a moment to figure out how it all worked, but gradually I gathered that people walked around until they saw either a fabric or a garment they liked. From there, the fun began.

Initially, much of what I saw had no bearing on what I wanted. A former fashion designer acquaintance had drawn out a picture of what I had in mind—a tailored shirt with princess seams and French cuffs. Armed with my sketch, I was ready to go. But everywhere I looked I saw silk sarongs and shapeless shifts. Nothing cotton or tailored in sight—until, out of the corner of one eye, I glimpsed a gorgeous puce-colored silk jacket. If this tailor could make something so beautiful, surely they could manage a simple blouse.

The tiny booth I had chosen was crammed with bolts of gorgeous silk—elegantly patterned or subtly colored ones that changed hues in the lights. Hanging above the fabric were many more styles of elegant jackets, dresses, and blouses. It was run by a tiny young woman deep in conversation with an East Indian lady just a bit older than me, who was having something made for her daughter. I listened in, eager to hear how this all worked. Soon, I was included in the conversation. Once she made her order, the lady kindly stayed on to help me negotiate mine.

I showed them my picture, and then I chose three or four thick cotton fabrics that I thought would suit my purposes. At this point I was ready to call it a day, until my new Indian friend leaned in and whispered, "You know, they can make anything here. You should get something special done."

I had had a childhood full of having special things made. The idea evoked the thought of endless sessions standing on a small stool being poked and prodded, which was not appealing at all. But not wanting to seem impolite, I took another look around and saw a jacket that was truly beautiful—pale grey silk embroidered with bronze and silver, cut in a feminine Nehru style.

"Well," I said, faltering, "maybe that one?"

The owner quickly pulled it down for me to try on. It was a bit too short in the sleeves and big in the bust, but she assured me she could make it fit my measurements. It was a flattering cut on me, and would certainly be a special memento of my trip to China.

Then something happened—I'm still not sure what. Was I channeling Mary Grant Price because I was in Shanghai? Or did a lifetime of training simply click into place? I morphed from a tentative American tourist buying a few travel keepsakes to a fashion maven exuding a confidence and knowledge base I had no idea existed within me. I began pulling down bolts of silk, various jackets, skirts and pants, suggesting combinations of colors and styles—with my new Indian friend chiming in enthusiastically and throwing in her own suggestions. In the end, I ordered 10 pieces—including cotton blouses, silk coats, jackets, and pants. (The total price was less than $600!) I had a blast!

There was only one hitch: I was leaving in 36 hours, and I was certain, given my Mrs. Williams experiences, that there was no way they would be finished in time. Surely I would have to return for a few fittings in order to get it right. But I was told that everything would be ready in 24 hours.

I arranged to get back to the booth by 3 PM the next day, which I figured would leave us two hours for any necessary alterations. When I arrived, everything was ready, packaged up beautifully. I undid each one, more excited than I had ever been at any Christmas, but prepared for my next unpleasant ordeal. One by one, I tried everything on. One by one, I realized that they not only fit, but they fit like they had been made for me, which, of course, they had been. Not one piece needed altering in any way. They were perfect!

After paying my balance, I gathered up my items and began walking out of the building, almost in a daze. Frankly, I couldn't believe it, and in my astonishment, I heard myself say, "Well, take that Mrs. Williams."

The moment those words came out of my mouth, I regretted them because the next thing I realized stunned me. I understood for the first time that all the poking and pinning and tucking and altering had had nothing to do with Mrs. Williams' skill at all. She had been as gifted a seamstress as any of these Chinese tailors.

As I walked out into the smoggy Shanghai sunshine, I suddenly realized that not only had she been patient to the point of long-suffering with a child who clearly had no appreciation for her endless labor on my behalf, but that she was also endlessly calm and non-reactive with my mother, who was used to running a team of Broadway and later Hollywood sewing rooms filled with eager young costumers hopping to it at her beck and call. Left to her own devices, I'm sure Mrs. Williams could have whipped up anything I had wanted and made it fit me with the same alacrity and finesse as this tailor had. She certainly had been able to make anything my mother wanted. The endless fittings and changes and do-overs, the fussing and primping and alterations that I had endured, I suddenly saw, had not been at the hand of Geneva Williams. It had all been my mother.

I kept having to go back to be refitted because my mother never could seem to get it right. Not the clothes—they were right enough. She couldn't get the clothes right on *me*. My mother was a costume designer, and I was her character. But no matter what she made for me, an immense chasm existed between the description of me that my mother carried in her head and the actual tomboy child being poked and prodded. The child whose wardrobe my mother was designing had never been me. It had been her idea of me, the me she wanted me to be, to look like—so I could become the woman she hoped I would become. The woman who would not only reflect well on her, but also live her life forward carrying the best of her bravery without the worst of her fears. She made me more and more clothes, hoping against hope that the adage would come true: The clothes would make me . . . into the person she wanted me to be.

The irony was, of course, that once, when she was young, my own mother had been ebullient and rebellious, too. The little girl who couldn't wait to kick off her shoes and run barefoot on the beach grew up into a free-spirited rebel who rode on the backs of motorcycles in short shorts and men's shirts tied up above her tan midriff, her platinum blonde–dyed hair whipping behind her in the wind. She was known for her risky fashion choices and willingness to try anything when it came to style. Unhappy with the hair dyes of her day, she set out to invent her own—and ended up with green hair! She didn't care. That just made for a great story.

Rebel though she might have been, however, my mother had grown up in the British caste system. Her colonial forebears—many of them well known in India and South Africa—had flourished, while her own father had taken his family into poverty. In Shanghai, she had seen the cosmopolitan world she wanted to live in, and she knew what it would take to get there: bravery, creativity, guts—and knowing how to fit in.

Like many immigrants, my mother saw America as the Promised Land. A place where you could reinvent yourself to be anyone you wanted to be. But to do that, you had to be able to play the part. My mother designed the costumes of her own imagined life. She figured out how to dress, look, speak, and act like the person she wanted to become. But inside, she always remembered who she was and where she had come from. It was a gift and a curse, the source of deep compassion for others like herself and of great insecurity for all the ways she judged herself not good enough.

But I, her daughter, could be different. I was born with the kind of privilege she could only try to fabricate for herself. So she made sure that I would never ever have the same experiences she had had of not knowing how to do the things that the people who had gone to Andover and Exeter, Harvard and Yale, knew how to do: dance, ski, play tennis, have table manners, read Tolstoy, know the right people, say the right things, wear the right clothes. I would become what she could only pretend to be.

She taught me that if I wanted to make it in the world, I had to look and sound the part. She believed that whether I understood it as a child or not, one day I would appreciate it all.

All those skills she made sure I was taught, all the right schools I attended, even the clothes I learned to wear—they *have* made a difference in my life. But at what cost to us both? The wound my mother bore was never feeling she was good enough. She believed that she could spare me that same wound. It didn't work. My mother's fear of her own inadequacies came to overshadow all the other gifts she had given me.

After being an assistant costume designer for eight years, my mother landed her first Broadway musical when she was 27 years old—Cole Porter's *Mexican Hayride*. After working on such legendary productions as *Oklahoma* and *Carmen Jones*, my mother was ready. Her designs were so spectacular that they overshadowed a somewhat lackluster production. The *New York Times* critic cleverly quipped, "I left whistling the costumes." It was the validation my mother had waited her whole life to receive.

I had spent my whole life whistling my mother's costumes. It was time for me to begin singing my own songs. Time for both of us to stop playacting and to love who we really were: imperfect, flawed, but always beautifully right. As the Chinese proverb says, "With time and patience, the mulberry leaf becomes a silk gown."

25

I SEE AND
I REMEMBER

As soon as I got to Shanghai, I pulled out my camera. Of all my joy practices, photography may be my most joyful. Wherever I go, I photograph anything and everything. My one directive: Don't think. Just click. I shoot whatever captures my eye, my heart, my soul, my mind, my spirit.

Carl Jung wrote, "Who looks outside, dreams; who looks inside, awakes." I look at the outside world when I photograph, but I look inside my soul when I see what pictures I have taken. I am usually surprised by what I have seen, and nowhere was this more true than in China.

That first day, I shot everything I saw without hesitation. That night in the hotel room, I downloaded my pictures and revisited my day: the colorful koi in a pond at a temple, ephemeral calligraphy written in water on a stone wall, ancient stones on garden floors in curvilinear shifting shapes. What I hadn't realized was that I had also been taking countless pictures of children with their grandparents.

One series in particular stood out: a grandfather at a temple teaching his grandson how to worship. I was struck in the moment by the idea that this man was the bridge between a legacy of spirituality that had almost been lost during Maoism, a legacy that he had not been able to pass down to his own children, but now could share with his grandson.

The next day I went out and explored the city in greater depth. When I got back to the hotel, I discovered I'd taken even more photographs of children with their grandparents. So it continued. Everywhere I went I was drawn to the children, always dressed in impossibly cute prints and patterns and colors in stark contrast to their drably dressed grandparents in Mao jackets.

Soon my guides knew to stop for me to have time to photograph them, and often they engaged the grandparents in conversation. The grandparents were always eager to show off their young charges—pointing at my camera, encouraging them to wave and smile, to say hello to me.

Upon returning home, I began editing my photos. The more I looked, the more I began to feel that a deeper message was calling to me.

My mother was also an inveterate photographer. Wherever we went, she took pictures, which she meticulously gathered into a series of large white photo albums. She safeguarded those albums as though they contained state secrets. I'm not kidding. My father, brother, and I knew that she kept incredibly detailed albums of our whole lives, but none of us ever saw them. Ever.

When I was writing my biography of my father, for the first time my mother gave me a guided and carefully edited tour of the photos she had deemed might hold useful pictures for the book. Still I only saw what she allowed me to see. It wasn't until after she died that I discovered she'd made thirty albums.

I decided I wanted to create some kind of ritual around looking at her photos, and so I made dinner plans for six of us—my partner and me, my brother and his wife, and Hank and Marin Milam, a couple who has been part of our family for as long as I could remember. After dinner, I pulled out the albums in chronological order, and we all sat around eager to see this treasure trove that contained the visual history of our lives.

As we began to flip through the pages, we saw pictures of all the places we had visited, our family, our friends, beautiful views, interesting buildings, animals, architectural details, trees, rocks, patterns. Photo after photo after photo—in almost too much detail. In fact, after about an hour, we all looked at one another and realized that our eagerness to see the albums had worn off. There were so many photos in such detail that we had lost interest.

We all felt the same way: We simply couldn't fathom what all the fuss had been about, and we didn't care to know. My brother packed the boxes up and put them in his attic, and none of us had any urge to look at them for a decade—until, that is, I came home from China, whereupon I found myself wanting to see what my mother had seen when she was behind the lens.

As I looked through her shots of the buildings, views, trees, and animals that had captured her eye, I realized not only were my mother and I drawn to many of the same subjects, but also, like me, she rarely let herself be photographed. She preferred being behind the camera—a camera she always had with her.

For the first time, I realized that my love of photography had come from her, that we both chronicled our lives in the same visual ways, and that we saw the world through very similar eyes.

I finally got why my mother had safeguarded her photo albums: They were the chronicle of her inner life. She never kept a journal. She recorded through her eyes. She knew that most of those photos would have meant nothing to anyone but her. They told her the story of her life. How she saw reminded her of how she had felt.

It was then that something else struck me. Something that stood me still and sat me down. I realized that my mother had had one favorite subject. One I did not have. A subject she photographed more than anything else—more than animals and architecture and beautiful views.

That favorite subject was us. My father and me. The people she loved.

My parents were 51 and 45 when I was born, the age of many of those grandparents I had photographed. In China, I thought I had been drawn to those grandparents because I longed for something those little children had—the unconditional love and undivided attention their grandparents were giving them. When I went through my mother's photo albums after coming back from China, I saw something else.

In my favorite photo of my dad and me, I'm about three or four. We're framed by the back door of our motor home. We're both wearing white and his arms are wrapped around me, his face lit up with joy. Nestled safely, I have a quiet smile that comes from feeling utterly loved. It's the only photo I have always kept framed on my desk.

Over the years, that photo always reminded me how much my dad and I loved one another. It took me going to China and leaving my old stories of my mother there to return home seeing her through my newly opened lens of Love. Only then could I see that there are three people who loved each other in that photograph. Only then could I see just how much the third person—the one holding the camera—loved me, too.

26

AUTHORED BY MARY *AND* VINCENT PRICE

The year after I returned from China, Dover Publications reached out to me with an offer to reissue my parents' world-famous cookbook, *A Treasury of Great Recipes* by Mary and Vincent Price. I was thrilled to be a part of this fiftieth anniversary edition of a book that had become not only one of the most iconic American cookbooks, but one of the top ten out-of-print books of all time! I had only one problem.

The publishers wanted me to write an extensive preface about my family's culinary history, but I didn't see how I could write anything positive about food at all. When my parents divorced in 1973, I was convinced that I was the cause. More specifically, I was convinced that my eating habits and table manners were the cause. Many kids who see their parents argue feel they are responsible for those marital discords. During my childhood, the only time I saw my parents fight was at the dinner table.

In the early years of their marriage, my mother was the better cook, my father the enthusiastic eater. The *Treasury* was a true collaboration between my parents. Its message of encouraging people to explore, savor, and celebrate their lives through food, design, and culture perfectly expressed their life philosophy.

After the book sold over 350,000 copies in the mid-1960s, my father was asked to share his culinary expertise on talk shows and other television programs, so he threw himself into learning everything he could about the culinary arts. He became a superb chef and a dedicated gourmet. My mother, who always prided herself on her rail-thin figure, found herself having to eat countless rich meals at gourmet restaurants all over the world. Three cookbooks and a very finicky child later, food often became as much a source of conflict as of joy for my parents.

On one of our last trips as a family in the early 1970s, we sailed on the QE2 to Europe and then drove all over the Loire Valley and Northern France. For days leading up to our excursion to Mont St. Michel, all my parents could talk about was the island's world-famous restaurant, which apparently had the best omelets in the world. This was not good news for me. I loathed omelets. An omelet restaurant held about as much appeal to me as going to summer school to learn long division.

For days leading up to our arrival at Mont St. Michel, my mom and dad had the same discussion: my mother, of the when-in-Rome camp, firmly espousing her belief that as I might never get the chance again, I should eat one of the most famous omelets in the world. My father, always on my side, countering with something like, "Let the girl be." In the end, as always happened, it was easier for my father and me to acquiesce to my mother's wishes. I ate the damn omelet. Then I spent the next two days throwing up all across Bretagne.

I threw up a lot as a child. Apparently, all that focus on food disagreed with me. I was the kid who longed to be taken to Bob's Big Boy for a burger and fries. The gastronomic delicacies of our world travels often produced rather indelicate results in my digestion. But far worse than my intolerance for certain foods was my mother's intolerance of my table manners. I slumped. I shoveled. I pushed things around my plate. I never remembered what fork went with which course. And when I wasn't trying not to eat what was set before me, I downed everything at Mach speed.

The real message I inferred about food from my mother was that food is dangerous. My mother believed that if you practically looked at a potato you could become overweight. I'm not sure a tuber of any kind ever entered our kitchen. Sweets were only for special treats. Bread, if it had to be consumed at all, was rationed like water in the desert. By the time I got to high school, my mother had taken to making my school lunch sandwiches on something called Pepperidge Farm Very Thin Bread. That was an overstatement. Microscopic was more like it. By lunchtime, whatever filling had once been in the sandwich had seeped through the bread. All I had left to eat was a soggy lump of beige ooze.

I was always a tall skinny kid. I didn't break 100 pounds until I was in tenth grade and had almost reached my full 5'11". Yet I never saw myself as thin. In high school, I had to eat five or six times a day not to feel hungry—purloining anything my classmates did not want from their lunches or buying something off the lunch truck after finishing whatever my mother had packed. I snuck cookies and bags of chips from our pantry, hoping she wouldn't notice. Then I hated myself for it.

By the time I was a senior in college, I was anorexic, subsisting on a few Kit Kat bars each day in an effort to stay what I would have called "svelte." Although I eventually faced down the scourge of anorexia, food still felt dangerous. I monitored everything I put in my mouth for possible allergic reactions, and whatever I did eat, I consumed so quickly that I barely tasted it.

My lifelong relationship with food was never a good one. Now I was being asked to write about my family's iconic cookbook. I had to do something.

The answer came through loud and clear: *Take a road trip!*

⌒

I conceived the plan of eating my way around the country, piecing together an itinerary around some talks I had scheduled. I hoped to visit as many of the original restaurants that had been featured fifty years earlier in the original cookbook as possible. The city with the most mentions was New Orleans, which was conveniently en route to my first speaking gig in Atlanta.

New Orleans was the American city I was least interested in visiting. I pictured it as a party town full of big drinkers and small talkers with some spooky voodoo thrown in. Now even my reticence to go to NOLA seemed perfect. It gave me the opportunity to change two old stories—one about food and the other about New Orleans. Then I realized my travel dates fell during Mardi Gras. The idea of spending three days in a city full of inebriated revelers seemed hideous. But I had no choice. So I cajoled my intrepid friend Cynthia into joining me just for the New Orleans part of my adventure, and off we went.

Within a few hours of our arrival, I—the last person who would have ever visited New Orleans during Mardi Gras—had changed her mind completely. On our way to our first cookbook lunch, Cynthia and I found ourselves stuck in a human traffic jam of body-painted people in various states of undress on Bourbon Street. I heard someone yell down at me, and when I looked up at the balcony above, guys were tossing down Jell-O shots, one of which I caught one-handed (with my left hand no less!) to great applause. I gave my Jell-O shot to the sweaty stranger next to me, Cynthia and I exchanged a hilarious high-five, and from then on, I just went for it all.

I ate everything from a piping hot beignet at Café du Monde (even though in my "real life" I have been gluten-free for over a decade, and sugar-free and dairy-free since my twenties) to fried alligator, cheese grits, and countless calorie-rich dishes swimming in Béchamel sauce. I loved every single bite! In fact, at the end of our first meal, the two gentlemen who had been dining at the table next to us came over and asked whether Cynthia and I were food critics. We must have looked confused, because one of them said, "It's just that you were so freaking *into* that meal!"

I was so freaking into *all* of Mardi Gras. I—the shy teetotaler in the corner at every party, who can't imagine what I could possibly have to say to anyone in the room—loved that everyone leaves both their inhibitions and their sobriety at home at Mardi Gras. Every bar door, balcony, and city stoop was filled with revelers or watchers, shouting out their welcome. On every street corner, drummers, tuba players, washboard strummers, and bluegrass bands filled the air with musical invitations to throw cares and inhibitions to the wind and join in the Mardi Gras joy. We did!

The one thing I had no intention of doing during Mardi Gras was going to a parade. But when Cynthia and I realized how much fun we were having, we decided to check out the beginning of the Bacchus Parade. The moment I saw the first marching band and float, I was hooked! We ended up staying right to the end. Festooned with beads, we walked back to our B&B well after midnight on streets spilling over with people rife with post-parade enthusiasm.

I felt as though I had undergone a religious conversion: I had spent a lifetime avoiding Mardi Gras like the plague, only to discover that, done right, it is a mecca for joy and a reminder that everyone—even (or maybe especially) workaholic uptight WASPs like me—needs to remember to make time to play.

The joy of Mardi Gras set the tone for my whole trip. Cynthia flew home, while I made my way east, sharing delicious meals with old friends all along the way. For the first time in my life, I began seeing food as a conduit for connection instead of as either a problem or a temptation. I recognized that the real recipes in any cookbook are for the joy in every encounter, the adventure possible in every meal, and the deep communion with the people with whom you break bread. All of my old stories about food began to be replaced by the joy I experienced in every new encounter. So it came as a total surprise when on the night I drove into Boston—one of the cities my mother called home for the last quarter century of her life—I burst into tears as the skyline came into view. I was flooded with intense and unexpected emotion.

The next day, I decided to have lunch at the Museum of Fine Arts. From the time we began visiting Boston together while I was still in high school, and for the next twenty-five years, my mom and I often ate at their formal dining room. I hadn't been there in at least 15 years, but it was just the same—its muted taupe color scheme matching the muted taupe winter courtyard below. Being in that elegant room, I was filled with a sweet nostalgia.

As I enjoyed my clams in white-wine-and-butter sauce, I suddenly felt flooded with gratitude for my mom. I realized for the first time that without her discipline, her metaphysical underpinnings, her high standards and follow-through, her tough love, her refusal to coddle or enable me as yet another celebrity child, I wouldn't have made it.

When my life fell apart, when I disappointed myself over and over again, when I failed and failed again and failed better, it was my mother in me who never let me give up. The discipline and backbone she had instilled in me through her tenacious love had kept me alive. Until that afternoon in the museum, I hadn't recognized the fundamental role my mother had played in my survival.

While my father's Renaissance soul has translated itself into the many passions that are the high notes of my existence, my mother became my rhythm section—the bass line that grounds me. My whole life, my loving focus had always been on my dad. Because I adored my father, I had made him the sole hero of my story. That left my mother to become the villain who voiced all of my darkest fears and doubts. By learning to see all the ways my mother was like me, by having compassion for her fears and forgiving all the failings in her that looked so much like my own, I could finally recognize how much she had loved me, and I her.

It took coming to Boston to bridge both parts of me, to acknowledge that, like *A Treasury of Great Recipes*, I, too, was authored by Mary *and* Vincent Price.

By the end of that three-week road trip, gone was my epic tale of gustatory woes, replaced by a beautiful understanding of what it really means to break bread with friends, family, and strangers alike. The preface to the cookbook wrote itself with ease. Far more importantly, however, gone was the lifelong fable I had spun of my mean mother. I felt a kind of freedom I never knew existed.

When one door closes, another always opens. As I released my mother, I crossed a threshold into another journey of forgiveness—this time with someone I never realized I needed to forgive. I came face to face with my father.

27

FOLLOWING THE
WRONG GOD HOME

In a photograph I took when I was about seven years old, my mother and father are sitting side by side at a tiny restaurant table—one yellow rose between them. They are both looking out at the world, both seeing the same thing. My father's expression is one of sheer and utter delight. My mother looks stricken, like she wishes she were anywhere but there. When I saw it, I just wanted to go back in time, give her a big hug, and tell her everything really was okay.

In that picture, one of my parents was filled with joy and the other numb with terror. When I vowed to change my life, I asked myself: Which legacy was I going to choose? Expansion or contraction? Love or fear? Curiosity or judgment? Openness or rigidity? I chose to expand into love. To do that, I had to keep cracking my heart open in forgiveness.

We can never truly forgive until we learn how to love, just as we can never truly love until we learn how to forgive. In order to forgive by loving and love by forgiving, each of us must, as August Wilson so beautifully expressed it, "Confront the dark parts of yourself, and work to banish them with illumination and forgiveness. Your willingness to wrestle with your demons will cause your angels to sing."

I had been wrestling with my mother's demons for as long as I could remember. It wasn't until I forgave her that I could see something that had always eluded me: I needed to wrestle with my father's demons too, if I ever wanted to finally hear my angels sing.

I was, still am, and always will be a Daddy's Girl. Being a Daddy's Girl is something you never grow out of. At least I never have. My father remains the person I have loved the most in the whole wide world.

People often ask me when I realized my famous father was not like other people. That question always perplexed me until I understood why it didn't make sense. I never thought my dad wasn't like other people because he was famous. I thought he was famous because he wasn't like other people.

My dad *wasn't* like other grownups. When he walked into a room, it was as though the whole roof blew off and the sun shone down illuminating us all. He was one of the brightest lights I have ever met.

Everything we did together was so much fun—and not all the stuff you might think. Sure it was incredible to visit movie sets or travel first class to London or see the Eiffel Tower or ski in Switzerland. But that's not what I really remember best from my childhood.

I remember sitting on the beach sifting through stones as we tried to find the smoothest ones for skipping. I remember doodling on paper placemats together in diners. I remember sitting on his lap while he told me about the Big Dipper and Orion's Belt. I remember sharing Tootsie Rolls and root beer floats on a road trip. I remember just holding his hand and feeling like there was nothing that would ever feel as safe and loving and glorious as being with him. When people told me that I looked just like my dad, I was so proud—not because I wanted to look like a bearded horror movie actor in his mid-50s, but because looking like my dad meant looking like pure lit-up joy!

As a little girl, I modeled myself on all the qualities I loved about my dad—his joy, his enthusiasm, his generosity of spirit, his appetite for life. He was the person I loved most in the whole wide world. I just wanted to be like him. It was that simple. As long as I held onto the thread of my father's joy, anything felt possible.

We all have a thread that connects us to the truth of ourselves. When we lose the thread, we feel unmoored, adrift, because we have lost our innate connection to our own hearts. My thread connecting me to my father, to my heart, and to the world had always been joy, but somewhere along the way I began to lose it. By the time I was in my twenties, I nearly lost it for good.

⌒

While my true self had always known that joy was what connected my heart to my father's heart and to the heart of the world, my false self had hitched its wagon to the star of his fame. When you grow up the kid of a celebrity, no matter what you do, fame remains a fact of your life. As a little girl, I never noticed that people treated me differently because I had a famous father. As I grew older, however, I both detested the smallness of that hypocrisy and craved the way it sometimes made me feel special. I began to look on my dad's stardom as something that I either desired or despised, and my minor celebrity as something either tantalizing or terrifying. I lost the simple thread of joy that had connected me to my father, by getting lost in the story of his fame. It wasn't until I found myself on the Way of Being Lost that I realized celebrity had been my greatest red herring.

By focusing on his fame, I had forgotten something so fundamental about my father. What I had always most admired, envied, and wished to emulate was my dad's immense generosity of spirit. In everything he did, he gave back. He used his fame to inspire and encourage others to live their best lives. *That* was the source of his joy. *That* was what gave his life meaning and purpose. And *that* was what had been missing in my own.

I had never felt like I had shown up to my best life as my truest self because I had never found a way to feel anything other than selfish. To me, to live a life of meaning meant to give something back. I had lost sight of what I had always known as a child—that my dad was not special because he was famous, but rather that he was famous because he made other people feel special. I began following the wrong god home.

Once I grasped this thread of his joy again, I wasn't about to let it go. But to do that—just as I had with my mother—I had to unearth and expunge some life-limiting narratives that had blocked my truth and killed my joy. Stories this time that had come from my father.

Just like me, my dad had also struggled to believe that he deserved all the good he had been given. He felt guilt that his older brother had been forced to give up his own dreams to work in the family business—a path that led my uncle away from his heart, into the bottle, and eventually to an early death of cirrhosis of the liver.

Just like me, my dad was a workaholic. I knew that he worked as hard as he worked, gave as much as he gave, because his false self also tried to tell him he didn't deserve what he had received.

Also like me, my father abdicated his power to strong women, and fought off his own feelings of never having shown up to his own life.

But unlike me, my father had used his life to be of service to the world. Although he, too, spent long nights in the darkness of his own soul, unlike me, he had never stopped shining his light. Now it was time to shine mine.

The word "celebrity" connotes a celebration of a person's achievement. Celebration and joy are intimately connected. As John O'Donohue reminds us: "There's something really holy in real celebration. Real celebration is about the lyrical dance of joy at the center of the human heart."

I saw that in both blaming and blessing my dad for his celebrity, I had made fame far too important. Fame kept my father on a pedestal in my head instead of in joy in my heart. Fame also let my father off the hook for all the ways he hadn't shown up in my life. By letting him off the hook, I kept myself on it. Instead of reckoning with and accepting his imperfections, I took their whole burden on myself.

I have come to understand that my father's fame was perfect for him. Fame was probably the *only* platform big enough for him to shine his light and to spread all the joy he exuded. What was right for my father was right for my father. Now I had to release myself from all of his old stories—the good, the bad, the ugly—if I was ever going to find what was right for me.

28

MY
CAMPHO-PHENIQUE

A year after my father fell in love with Coral Browne, she moved into my dad's new house in the Hollywood Hills. When I came to visit, he told me that he had a new "houseguest." I was a pretty naive 12-year-old, so I believed him.

One evening in 1974, while I was waiting for my mom to get off the phone so I could ask her a homework question, I saw my dad's face flash on our television screen. As I moved closer, I heard the announcement that my father had married his "houseguest" that afternoon. I had a stepmother.

Coral was everything my mother wasn't. She knew she was gorgeous. She walked around the house naked after sunbathing, flaunting her beauty and her own audacity. She laughed loudly, socialized gladly, professed her acerbic opinions on everything, surrounded herself with her admirers, and left the mark of her indelible wit on everyone she met. She was also a remarkable actress—and like my mother, she was a brilliant businesswoman, a style innovator always ahead of her time.

In my 1999 biography of my dad, I wrote that I saw Coral as a cross between Cruella de Vil and Auntie Mame. That was the only way I could express the way Coral's inexplicable cruelty paired with her completely infectious *joie de vivre*. Her total excision of my brother's two children from their grandfather's life is something I will never be able to explain or condone. Her love-hate behavior toward me was more mercurial—and therefore so much more confusing. I never knew which Coral I was going to get—the one who lent a sympathetic ear to my romantic troubles, or the one who could excoriate me with curse words I never even knew existed.

One Sunday evening when I was 27, I came home from a weekend trip to a friend's ranch to find a message from her on my answering machine. "Your dad is in hospital," Coral said tersely in her inimitable Aussie/British drawl. "The doctors don't know what's wrong with him, and it isn't looking good. But don't bother trying to find him. He's under an assumed name. I'll call you if you need to know anything." Click.

I will always remember the complete helplessness I felt. This was my dad, the person I loved most in the world. He might be dying, and I couldn't see him? My emotions careened from sadness to rage to helplessness. I knew there was nothing I could do. This was the wife he had chosen. He had rarely if ever stood up to her when he was well, and he certainly didn't have the strength to do it now.

It wasn't that I didn't understand Coral. Even as a teenager, I could see that underneath all her panache and bravado, she was an incredibly fearful person. I could palpably *feel* her fear.

In his eulogy for her, the actor Alan Bates captured it best: "We all knew Coral Browne, the superb actress—witty, stylish, powerful, classical, and of course beautiful. We all knew the Coral Browne that she presented to us socially—a great personality, mischievous, alarming, unpredictable, outrageous. There is another less well-known Coral Browne. I was invited to present her with an Evening Standard Award. When she came to the stage, suddenly the supremely confident Coral Browne was nervous and vulnerable. I think the reason why we all loved her was perhaps because we all sensed that underneath her wicked sense of humor was this vulnerability, and it made all her outrageousness wonderfully acceptable."

When people bring up Coral to me now, almost 25 years after her passing, I've noticed something I've come to refer to as "the Coral wince." Even if I'm not face to face with them, I can feel it . . . a kind of psychic hesitation, a discomfort with all the contradictions of Coral. It happens with people who knew her and loved her, as well as with people who were treated badly by her.

Even Coral's dearest friends recognized that she was, by her very nature, a two-edged sword—a barbed rapier wit with one of the truest and kindest hearts on the planet. The Coral wince is an admission of discomfort by people filled with admiration and love for an extraordinary woman, whose legacy was colored by her fear, anger, and dishonesty. The Coral wince is also a kindness directed toward me, because Coral was my wicked stepmother for eighteen years.

The first time I felt the Coral wince came when her biographer Rose Collis interviewed me in 2006 and hesitatingly asked, "How does it feel to be talking about her?"

Fine, I thought. I really had no idea what Rose meant. Then she asked, "Have you been able to forgive her?"

That surprised me, because I had begun forgiving Coral a few weeks after she passed. If forgiveness releases the stories we keep repeating about people or situations in our past—stories that do nothing but keep us trapped in cycles of shame, guilt, and fear—I thought, *Coral is dead and I am alive. Which one of us is going to suffer if I don't forgive her?* All I had really ever wanted was for her to love me and let my dad and me love one another. Her death allowed both of those things to happen.

Forgiveness is a lifelong process, never a one-off deal. Forgiveness with Coral has remained a gradual untangling of the snarls and stories that keep me from seeing my wicked stepmother through the eyes of love. To view Coral from that place of love, I had to learn to see her as my father did.

When my dad married my mother in 1949, she had been a free and joyful person, an iconoclast and fashion maven much like Coral. But over the 23 years of my parents' marriage, my mother had contracted into greater and greater fear and rigidity, overwhelmed by what became a sense of duty and responsibility—her sense of obligation to my dad's image and to our family legacy, which she felt the need to protect and grow. My father felt that keenly; it crashed up uncomfortably against his innately joyful and free nature. So when Coral came into his life, my father fell head over heels in love. Coral's insouciant fuck-it-all attitude helped return him to his joy.

The first years of their marriage brought out the best in both of them. Even I could see that. However, Coral Browne had underestimated Vincent Price's fame. She had partnered with a man whose bright light she hoped would ignite her own, because the death of her first husband had plunged her into a mesmeric terror of her own death that she seemed unable to shake. When my father's immense light outshone hers, Coral tried to rein him in under the guise of protecting him, just as my mother had done. She clamped down on everything and everyone he loved. Soon my father found himself hiding things from her, including his close relationships with his own children.

My father abhorred conflict. He told me how much he loathed it when Coral picked at me and I fought back. He told me, "After you and Coral have an argument, she forgets it right away. But you're like an elephant. You never forget." He asked me to make his life easier by forgiving Coral, so I tried, but Coral would invariably find another good reason to get angry at me.

It was one thing to have a mercurial wicked stepmother whose anger surfaced like a summer thunderstorm—loudly, violently, unexpectedly—only to be followed by a glorious sunset as though the storm had never even happened. It was another to have her change my relationship with my father.

When my parents were married, my dad had always taken my side. He was my hero, my champion. Now he was asking me to make his life easier by not fighting back when Coral poked at me. I loved him so much that I tried to do that, even though a little voice inside me kept saying, *You're my dad. I'm your daughter. Aren't you supposed to be doing this for me?*

Coral's biographer Rose gave me one of the great gifts of my adult life when she revealed that, to a person, all of Coral's friends had told her how badly they thought my stepmother had treated me. As a kid, I thought no one noticed. As a kid, I thought it was all my fault. Rose's revelation that other people noticed how badly she treated me and actually seemed to care about what was happening to me was huge! For the first time, I didn't feel crazy.

⁓

A few years after my stepmother's death, my father and I were in the car one day when he suddenly turned to me and said, "I'm sorry I wasn't a very good father."

I knew that my father meant what he said. I also knew that on some level it was true—he hadn't always been a very good father, even at the same time as he'd been the best father in the whole wide world.

He had been the person who taught me unconditional love—but he had also abandoned me to live with a woman whose fear had sometimes stifled her own ability to love.

My dad left me with my mother, whom he knew to be rigid and controlling and afraid and tough—while he went off to live with a woman whom he knew treated me terribly. He never stood up to either of them, and he never copped to any of it.

Worse, actually. A few years after my parents' divorce, my father decided to surprise Coral by converting to Catholicism. When he was told that being divorced might hinder that, he dispatched two priests to the house where my mother and I were living with this request: Would she consider annulling their marriage to facilitate his conversion? When my mother said no, he sent them back a second time. My parents had been married for 23 years, and I was their only child. Not only did he want to erase his marriage to my mother, but he also was willing in the process to then make me officially illegitimate.

Now, many years later, he was acknowledging his failings as a father to me. I knew that he wanted neither absolution nor forgiveness, but rather for me to hold him to the same tough scrutiny to which he held himself. From time to time, my father showed my brother and me his deepest doubts and fears. He worried that he had only skimmed the surface of life, had never let his heart fully open to anyone, had helped only himself. I understood that only my honest seeing could allow him to release himself from the self-loathing he, too, carried.

Like me, my father's self-hatred always stemmed from having failed his own standards of loving. The more we love, the greater our remorse when we do not love well. My dad was the person I have loved most in my life. I know that love was mutual. At the end of his life, my dad needed the daughter he loved so dearly to acknowledge his failings in order to set him free. I was too young to be able to give him what he needed. That too-young me still needed to keep the fiction of her father intact.

"Oh that's not true at all," I immediately responded to his admission. "You were a wonderful father. I love you." Because, of course, that was true, too.

It wasn't until I forgave my mother that I knew how to finish the conversation my father and I started in the car all those years ago.

For the first time, even if it was only in my mind, I could tell my father that I knew that he failed over and over again. I knew it because I, too, have failed, over and over again. I could tell him that I knew that he never lived up to his own expectations of himself and that he abandoned those he loved the most, especially himself. I know that because I, too, have never lived up to my own expectations of myself, and I, too, have abandoned those I loved the most, especially myself. I could tell him that he was imperfect, flawed, unreliable, fearful, and sometimes even mean. I know that because I, too, am imperfect, flawed, unreliable, fearful, and sometimes even mean. But I could also tell him again that I love him—not just despite the fact that he was all those things, *but because of them*.

My dad had one surefire remedy for everything. From a scrape to a stye, a toothache to a tummy ache, a corn to a concussion, he believed there was no ill that could not be cured by a stinky tincture called Campho-Phenique. He never left home without one of those tiny green bottles.

My Campho-Phenique is Forgiveness.

If, as Rebecca Solnit believes, "Roads are a record of those who have gone before," we have to be willing to retrace our steps to find our way back to where we started. That means not only releasing old hurts, but also being willing to stop idolizing someone we love so that we can finally see their warts, wounds, *and* wonderfulness.

The Way of Being Lost is, as much as anything, a story of forgiveness—releasing the past into the presence of Love. When we wrestle with our old demons so that we can see everyone as their own true self, at last we cause our angels to sing. Then, as we move beyond our old road maps, we begin to create new cartographies of hope.

PART SIX

SEEING THE TREASURES THAT PREVAIL

I came to explore the wreck.
The words are purposes.
The words are maps.
I came to see the damage that was done
and the treasures that prevail.
—Adrienne Rich

29

MAPPING
MY LIFE

I was the small triangular yellow flag pinned to the large world map hanging on the wall above the bed in my sunny bedroom in the home where I grew up.

My father, mother, and half-brother were blue, green, and red on that same map—the one place the four of us were always together during my childhood.

As the yellow flag, I was mostly stuck in Los Angeles. The red flag, my half-brother, had staked its claim in Albuquerque. Four years before I was born, Barrett had gone there for college in self-chosen exile from the celebrity upbringing that he felt lucky to have escaped. Red rarely moved.

Green and blue, my mother and father, were in constant motion.

Whenever I received a postcard of a painting, a cute animal, an airplane, or a hotel with arrows pointing to Mommie and Daddy's room—the back covered with my father's flowing script and plastered with exotic stamps picturing rare birds or crowned kings and queens—I was allowed to stand on my bed as my nannies helped me figure out where to move blue and green. I traced my parents' path both on the map and in my mind.

I was nine years old when we moved out of that house and the map came down. But its imprint remained. As the years passed, green moved less, though my true blue father never ceased his restless roaming around the globe. As for yellow, I went on to leap from Denver to Chicago to New York, from London to Paris to Switzerland. By then, I had come to view myself and my family geographically—defined, as much as anything, by our places on the planet.

I had already begun imagining the future road trip of my own life.

⌒

Oslo, Bangkok, Kalamazoo, Peoria—I loved the places with the funniest names. London, Madrid, Rome, Venice—I pictured the day when I would find myself there, standing in the square covered with pigeons, which my father had told me he fed. Looking up at the huge stone lions with the crossed paws my mother said she loved. Someday, my father wrote, I will bring you here. Someday, my father wrote, we will visit together. I miss you, my father wrote. I can't wait to be here with you. Someday.

In the road trip of my life, I have been chasing that Someday for as long as I can remember.

I adored my peripatetic father, so I modeled what has become my own nomadic life on his wanderlust. I longed to see the world through his omnivorous gaze, learn the secrets that he carried in his curious mind, discover the treasures he told me about in story after story. In fact, my mania for motion, which has become the leitmotif of my life, derived less from our voyages to glamorous world capitals and far more from the pure joy I always found when my mother, father, our dogs, and I would clamber into our brown milk truck of an RV—heading toward places invisible on the known world of that map above my bed.

The best parts of my childhood were spent on the family trips to Native American reservations we visited for my father's work on the Department of the Interior's Indian Arts and Crafts Board, or stopping in the tiny towns between the national parks my mother longed to see. The unmarked empty spaces between the bigger dots became the glorious wide-open world where everything our lives were supposed to look like got magically forgotten, as we became a family fully present together in the beauty and infinite possibility of the road.

When we returned to Los Angeles, it was to the 9,000-square-foot Spanish mansion my parents called The Big House that served as their office, architectural project, museum, and entertainment venue as much as our home.

Resembling more of a Grand Hotel than anything else, it was filled with a whole cast of characters: all the litters of my mother's Standard Poodles; my Dad's beloved mutt Joe; my Skye terrier Paisley (who came and then went when her bad habits proved to outweigh her good); Puffie the pug; innumerable goldfish in three ponds; an ever-growing family of turtles; a passel of screaming peacocks; a rooftop dovecote of pigeons; a hexagonal aquarium of tropical fish; an aviary of colorful chatty parakeets; our houseman, Harry; our laundress, Olean; my Uncle Hank; my nanny of the moment; Dad's secretary, Wawona; a security guard named Vic; and of course my sometimes-present father and my always-busy mother.

On the road, all that fell away.

My mother's miraculous metamorphosis—from self-appointed taskmaster of our lives to fellow traveler—took place the moment we left the L.A. city limits. My dad remained, as ever, our driver. Literally, figuratively, and metaphorically. His infectious enthusiasm for every single thing fueled, guided, and carried us through every journey. I was the navigator, neck massager, and convenient excuse for any childlike adventure and delicious detour, my mom the photographer, the nature lover, the awed observer of every glorious vista. Each with our self-chosen roles, together as equals.

We roamed far and wide—on and off the beaten track. Through obscure museums, past picture-postcard vistas, into one-stop-sign towns with silly names, and along endless stretches of empty road. My mom, my dad, our dogs, and me. Together. Away from constantly ringing telephones, fancy clothes, the never-ending letters-needing-responses world of movie people.

Out there, on the road, we met real folks who lived in a real world of cornfields and horse ranches and diners. Out there, on the road, *we* felt like real folks who lived in a real world of family and friendship and fun. Out there, on the road, where I felt like my truest self, I found home. Out there, on the road, I lived in Love and left fear in our rearview mirror. This was where my joy thrived.

30

CARTOGRAPHIES OF SILENCE

've always remembered those road trips as the happiest times of my childhood. I felt as though I were being introduced to Blue Sky America, our Big Beautiful Country into which I had been lucky enough to be born.

It was the nostalgic promise of that Blue Sky Big Beautiful Country that called me back out onto the road the summer after I turned 23. But only a few hundred miles down the Interstate, I realized that things didn't feel the same.

In 1985, America was struggling. So was I. Farmers were losing their land. Wall Street might have been flourishing in those Reagan years, but the American middle class was not. Driving the back roads through rural small towns in states I had never seen—Arkansas, Tennessee, North Carolina—I witnessed the disappearing middle-class neighborhoods, the anxiety of farm communities, the unhealed splits between black and white, the growing stratification between poor and rich. There was a national angst that seemed to mirror my own internal confusion. America felt a lot like I did: We were watching our familiar landmarks get boarded up, graffitied over, and plowed down, with no idea what would replace them.

That summer, I drove cross country and back in my baby blue 1963 convertible VW bug with my partner Sam and our two large dogs for the ostensible reason of attending the 90th birthday party of Sam's Italian-American New Jersey grandmother, whom I'd never met. Two months on the road. Two revelatory life-changing months. More than just a road trip, that summer was an awakening.

Six months earlier, I had dropped out of the prestigious graduate school in acting to which I had been accepted right out of college. From childhood on, I had wanted to be an actor like my dad, but by my early twenties, I had begun to feel more passionate about social justice than I did about the theatre. After I came out to my mom and she had rejected me, I felt even more called to do something that could help the world and not just me. Since I didn't yet know what that would look like, I decided to move to Albuquerque to be near my brother. Having jettisoned all the plans I had been making for myself since childhood, I craved the safety of someone I loved and who I knew loved me.

I got a job working on a horse ranch by day, and I baked 250 loaves of five different kinds of organic whole-grain bread by myself on late-night shifts at a cooperative bakery—which is to say, I was pretty lost. My whole life I thought I was going to be an actress. Now I had no idea what I was going to do. So I decided to take a few classes at the university that happened to be right up the street from the bakery.

That's where I met and began dating Sam—a smart, intense, deeply political, New Jersey-raised, Italian-American Women's

Studies professor eleven years my senior. Sam lived in a log cabin without running water or heat, drove an old VW van in which she loved to camp, and had a fluffy caramel-colored mutt named Sage, who was possibly the sweetest—and certainly the dumbest—dog I have ever met.

On our summer road trip, Sage, Sam, and I were joined on our adventure by Polo—a true trickster coyote—a German Shepherd mix, who had adopted me when he showed up at the horse ranch. I named him after Marco Polo, another fellow wanderer. Like his namesake, Polo had a penchant for wandering off and returning with amazing "gifts"—the dismembered haunch of a dead deer, for example. Hilariously, given his name, he also adored swimming pools—which was how he ended up swimming laps in Conway Twitty's pool after hopping out of the car at Twitty City to go on a little walkabout. Thank God for Polo, who provided the comic relief in our summer road trip movie! We sure needed it.

Sam and I could not have led more antithetical lives. I was a rich kid from a very famous family who had no clue just how different my childhood had been from 99.9 percent of the other people on the planet. I was also 23 years young, though I didn't know that either. Having always spent far more time with grownups than with people my own age, I was mentally precocious, which I equated with maturity. Although my head might have been smart, my heart hadn't yet entered preschool. I had never been in a long-term relationship. I had no idea what I was doing. And I had certainly never met anyone like Sam.

Sam had gone through some really tough experiences in her life. She had developed a quiver of learning resources, healing techniques, self-care strategies, and coping mechanisms, which I was eager to have her share with me. The books she read, the people she knew, the ideas she had developed about how the world worked blew my mind. I loved learning from her. But she had one coping mechanism she rarely let anyone see. When something really scared her, she soothed herself in a cocoon of solitude. The problem was that I was often what scared her, which meant that her go-to form of self-care felt to me as though she pulled away in times of stress and difficulty.

That summer, as we began to experience the differences between us in our conversations, in the ways we moved through the world, in how we spent money, in what brought us joy, Sam often retreated. Sometimes that meant sleeping in her own tent when we camped out; other times it meant that we spent days together in the car in near silence. When she was finally able to share what had made her withdraw, it was almost always something I had said or done that had triggered and scared her—which, in turn, triggered and scared me. There we were, two women who hardly knew one another and had precious little in common, traveling across country with our two dogs, freaking each other out. It was not the road trip I had imagined.

~

It was the silence that did me in. When I was a very little girl, the punishment I feared the most was being sent to my room to have dinner alone. I think my mother thought I hated that punishment because I wasn't with other people. That wasn't what I hated at all.

When I ate dinner alone sitting at my desk, I faced a huge plate glass window that overlooked a courtyard below. At night, everything outside was pitch black, so all I could see was a reflection of myself and the room behind me. I stared at my own unhappy face until I couldn't stand it anymore. Then I forced myself to look at my bedroom behind me.

There was a door at the far end of the room that opened onto a long upstairs hallway. It was always left cracked partway open. I would stare at that door and quake in fear. I was convinced monsters lurked just beyond that door. I sat there in the eerie silence of my lonely room knowing I could never cry for help, and waited for the monsters to come.

On that summer road trip, every time Sam pulled away, I felt like that little girl sitting in dreaded anticipation, knowing there was no one I could ask for help. My mother had rejected me and my sinful lifestyle, and I was all alone camping in the middle of nowhere with a woman I barely knew who sometimes didn't speak to me for days. In the silence, I waited for the monsters to come.

That summer, they did. The monsters in my head told me that I really was a sinner. That I had rejected the one person who had always been there for me—my mother—and now I really was all alone. They told me that I had abandoned everything I had been given—my life of privilege, my education, my friends. For what? To find my true self? To find my purpose? The monsters mocked me with their questions. The silence all around me was deafening. I heard no answers. There was no help. I was terrified.

That summer, I felt afraid in a way I never had before. What was I really afraid of? Everything and nothing, as we all are when we are caught in fear's clutches. What feels like the weight of the world when we are in it, we know to be flimsy mirages when we are not. I had heard fear's arguments for years. I had felt fear's icy claws scrape across my heart. But I had never experienced fear at its persuasive best until that summer road trip with Sam.

In twenty three years of a mostly lonely life, I had never felt so alone, so afraid, or so vulnerable. As I stood at the threshold between childhood and adulthood, fear had me in its clutches. Now that the monsters had finally come, they had no intention of letting me go.

⁓

Thank God some part of the joy-filled, hopeful younger me remained. My Inner Pollyanna. She still surfaced from time to time that summer, and when she did, how I loved her!

I still do. I think we all need a Glass Half Full Girl as our internal co-pilot, running down every rainbow not only for the pot of gold she is sure she'll one day find, but also for the sheer joy in smiling at that shimmering, many-colored arc of light.

The younger Pollyanna Me believed that every problem could be solved with a positive attitude, money I didn't always have, and overcoming the things that felt unfeelable by summoning a storybook spirit of adventure that could sew a silver lining on anything— transforming difficulty into a tale for the future. My Glass Half Full Girl soothed every fear-filled freakout that summer as best she could.

Mostly, though, she spent a lot of time looking out the window as this brave new world rolled by. What she saw ultimately became the whole reason I remember that trip.

In the end, it was not all the monsters that surfaced through the silence of that summer that stayed with me. The true treasure that prevailed from that road trip was the wildflowers.

31

WILDFLOWERING

Everywhere Sam and I drove on that summer road trip I saw them. Wildflowers blooming in reds and yellows, oranges and purples. Some more delicate, lithe and tall. Others multi-petaled and enormous. The flouncy ones and the sturdy, the scruffy and the hardy, the interplay of all their colors, shapes, and sizes—every one of them beautiful, joyful, life-affirming, and hopeful. I loved, loved, *loved* those wildflowers!

There was only one problem. They bloomed not off in some photo-worthy field underneath picturesque blue skies surrounded by scenic forests. Oh, no. They always seemed to bloom right by the side of the road. There where the asphalt pushed up against dirt, littered with old pop cans and discarded diapers, plastic bags and cigarette butts. That's where the wildflowers bloomed—and in riotous, gorgeous profusion.

No matter how much I sometimes don't want to be, I am my mother's daughter. I was raised to believe that beauty can only really be beauty if not a hair is out of place. So mile after mile

I saw the wildflowers and mile after mile they brought me joy. Yet all the while I hated the tarmac and litter for ruining the perfection of their beautiful blooms.

One day I found myself in conversation with a state park ranger in Arkansas. I mentioned how much I loved all the wildflowers along the side of the road before joking, "Don't they know how much prettier they'd look in some scenic field instead of surrounded by trash?"

My humor was lost on Ranger Rick, who earnestly replied, "Wildflowers always grow best where the soil is disturbed."

For the rest of the summer, I thought about that idea. I journaled about it. I even wrote a poem about it. Slowly but surely I came to realize that, of course, I loved those wildflowers because those wildflowers mirrored me.

Long after that summer ended, the ranger's words have stayed with me. Actually, I think about them pretty much every day: *Wildflowers always grow best where the soil is disturbed.* That sentence has become both my metaphor and my mantra.

⌒

In everything I have done creatively, everything I have written, everything I have taught, everything I have designed, what I eventually came to call My Wildflower Ethos has guided me and given me meaning when otherwise I might have given up hope of ever understanding myself. Whenever the space between my familiar false self and the mirage of the true me seemed hopelessly huge, My Wildflower Ethos taught me how to blossom right where I was.

That summer, when I saw those beautiful colors coming up in a place of seeming ugliness, when I learned that flowers need the disturbance of soil that happens when two seemingly disparate worlds bump up against one another, I realized that despite my mother's displeasure when anything seemed less than perfect, that messy place where unlikely things meet had always been the most compelling place for me to be. Exciting, energizing, interesting, fascinating, hopeful, healing—even as it is also uncertain, scary, unknown, confusing, and untidy— the disturbed soil between my false and true selves is where I've spent most of my life.

There—where the asphalt meets the dirt, where the litter of life accumulates and *still* the wildflowers grow—is the beautifully contradictory, completely unlikely, and fundamentally hopeful place where all necessary change begins. It is, in fact, the crucible of change (no matter how painful that change might initially be), and therefore the place where we must risk sowing the seeds of our deepest selves, our wildest dreams, and our greatest hopes. There, in that often uncomfortable wide-open liminal space between known and unknown, between fear and love, between hope and horror, between comfort and change, that is the space that we must be willing to inhabit in order to live the lives we seek.

When we inhabit liminal space, we are "occupying a position at, or on both sides of, a door, a boundary, or threshold." To be on both sides of something means that ultimately we find ourselves in neither. We are split, both inside and out. It is impossible to be present in either place—and we feel unsure of who we are because there is nowhere we fully belong. That place of in-between can feel like the place of greatest stress. Paradoxically—and therefore unsurprisingly—the greatest healing of my life has come when I recognize that these crevices of life are not places to fear, but rather spaces we must enter in willingness and joy.

The Irish poet John O'Donohue thought that thresholds are "a place where you move into more critical and challenging and worthy fullness . . . a line which separates two territories of spirit . . . How we cross is the key thing. If we cross worthily, what we do is we heal the patterns of repetition that were in us that had us caught somewhere. Then we cross on to new ground where we just don't repeat what we've been through in the last place we were."

In reality, crossing thresholds is actually all we are ever doing. We cross and repeat, cross and repeat. The challenge is to learn to see each threshold as another opportunity to leave behind the life-limiting narratives that no longer serve us, and so, eventually, to enter the territory of Spirit as our truest selves.

This is not always easy. With each threshold into a new territory of Spirit, we bring with us our false selves even as we seek to reunite with what is true.

In order to grow in grace, we must learn to resist the urge either to dump our past by the side of the road or to cling to long-tattered ideas we have outgrown. No more throwing the baby out with the bathwater or hoarding our stories long past their expiry dates. We must *both* release what no longer serves us *and* keep what we still need to grow in grace.

Our false selves would have us believe that we live in an either/or, us/them world in which we are continually urged to choose sides. Real life itself is far more fluid than this dualistic thinking would have us believe it to be. Only by learning to live in the space of both/and can we wildflower.

My whole life has been a wildflowering, *both* loving *and* fearing my fertile and fallow liminal spaces—seeding, growing, withering, blooming, scattering. Over and over again. In rainy times, watered by joy and creativity, hope and harmony, I have flourished alongside my fellow wildflowers as we arrayed ourselves in cheerful beauty, scattering our prolific joy to the winds and taking seed wherever we landed.

Of course periods of drought were inevitable when, scraggly and alone, I barely poked my head above the arid soil before withering away with the hope of trying again next season. And I would be less than honest if I didn't admit to the times when I desperately wished to be someone's cultivated fragrant flouncing rose, or their precious hothouse orchid solicitously tended and pruned, oohed and aahed over, pampered.

Still, I have always been a wildflower.

There are those who feel that wildflowers are weeds. Others call them volunteers, springing up in any opportune soil. Some might say they are botanical survivors, while many view them as floral carpetbaggers. I've thought of myself as all of them— these treasures that nevertheless persist and prevail no matter the disturbance or the damage. Only by wildflowering in the disturbed soil of my life have I finally been able to show up in the world as my truest self.

PART SEVEN

THE WAY OF BEING LOST

You've always had the power, my dear,
you just had to learn it for yourself.
—Glinda the Good Witch, *The Wizard of Oz*

32

Lions and Tigers and Bears, Oh My!

When I vowed to change my life in 2011, I had no idea what to do or how to do it, but I did have dreams—of living my calling, of moving through the world as my most authentic self, of learning how to love myself and others, of being of service and giving back to the world. To do that, I knew I needed to find a community with whom I could begin to share the kinds of conversations about inspiration and creativity, hope and healing I longed to have.

After my financial collapse, I had hidden myself away in shame. I cut myself off from old friends. I spent precious little time having fun and more and more time working. When I could no longer afford to do the things that had brought me joy-filled connection, like riding my horses, traveling, or taking classes—I saw that as just punishment for being such a financial fuck-up.

Fortunately, because I was able to keep my business open, I created meaningful relationships with my design colleagues, my employees, and my clients. But because our connection was work, I rarely let them see my personal struggles. I cut myself off from the pain in my heart, and let my head take over. The deep loneliness I felt inside is ultimately what led me to that wake-up call in the mirror.

As I began to show up to my own life, it became clear to me just how much I was craving a deeper kind of community. On my road trip back to my truest self, I needed brave companions beside me.

When I was a little girl, my mother and I watched *The Wizard of Oz* together on television every Thanksgiving weekend. Each year when the movie ended, I would turn to my mom and ask, "So it really was all a dream? Dorothy was asleep the whole time? She never even went to Oz?"

"Yes," my mother would tell me. "It was all a dream. Oz was in her head, and all the people in Oz were the people she saw around her every day. She thought she was away on a scary adventure, but all she had to do was wake up to realize she was home with everyone she loved the whole time." My first spiritual lessons came from watching *The Wizard of Oz* with my mom.

As I began to discover the Way of Being Lost, I realized that it looks suspiciously like that same spiritual yellow brick road. Your house gets blown away; your beloved dog gets taken; there are really, really wonderful people and really, really scary people and very pretty things that put you to sleep. But mostly there is the always-tempting belief that that someone out there who has magic powers can help you get home—if you can only find him and convince him to assist you.

Inevitably, of course, we all come to realize that the man behind that curtain is our false self, that home has always been

THE WAY OF BEING LOST

in our own hearts as our truest self, that we always end up where we need to go by the means we least hope to get there, and that no spiritual journey is ever possible without companionship. Just as Dorothy never would have found her way home without the Tin Man, the Scarecrow, and the Cowardly Lion, in order to find our way back home to our own hearts, we all need heart tribes.

As kids, we formed our heart tribes so easily because we lived from our hearts. As adults trained to go through life head first, we have to be willing to consciously and intentionally seek out and co-create community because healing cannot happen in a vacuum. We just have to be willing to find our heart tribes in unexpected places.

We have been educated to believe that our tribe should look like us—racially, ethnically, intellectually, politically, denominationally, or nationally. True tribes are built on the foundation of unconditional love. I found this out in what I thought were going to be scary dark woods filled with lions and tigers and bears. Oh my! I learned about heart tribes in the most unlikely of ways—from the horror community.

⌒

When I was first invited to attend a horror convention as Vincent Price's daughter and biographer, I thought the whole thing sounded nuts. First of all, I have never liked being scared. I couldn't imagine what kind of people could possibly want to spend an entire weekend celebrating fear. When I first started going to horror conventions and saw everyone walking around in costumes, wearing fake scabs, and covered in piercings and tattoos, I didn't know what to make of any of it. Who would want to slather blood all over themselves and stick a fake hatchet through their head?

It was my friend Jessie who helped open my eyes and heart when she told me something for which I will always be grateful: "You know how you always tell me that you've never fit in, always felt like an outsider? Well, so does everyone at this convention. But *they* get to go be with other people just like them, who love the same things they do. So don't worry that you don't fit in there. Go and celebrate that they have found a place where they can feel safe and loved among people who feel the same way they do!"

Horror conventions have taught me that deep, safe connection among like-minded people is not only possible, it is vital to living a life of joy. Buoyed by the safety of being with like-hearted people, we find the courage to love what and who we love—whatever it is and however we love it—and celebrate it together.

As I got to know horror fans, I realized that their costumes and makeup and tattoos and piercings were expressions of their truest selves. Horror fans, monster kids, and Goths have the courage to face the fears from which most of us hide—the fears they feel inside themselves as well as the fear they feel from others. There, in that disturbed soil, they wildflower into some of the most creative, kind, fun, honest, genuine, authentically interesting people I have ever met.

Although I may not *be* a horror fan, I have become a huge fan *of* horror fans—because the more time I have spent with them, the safer I feel being the authentic me. They model how to own your truest self and bring her out into the world in warts, wigs, weirdness, and wildness, wonder and all.

Eventually I got it. We were actually not so different, the horror fans and I. I just had to learn to see them through the lens of Love. I had to lose my belief that they were freaks and that I was not—that they were the fans and I was the "horror royalty." When I did, I saw that we are *all* monster kids—a community of people who have felt "different" in one way or another our whole lives. The ways in which we feel different don't really matter. Our differences may even make us seem different from one another. But that's the beautiful thing—whoever you are is fine!

Society doesn't celebrate outcasts. Society teaches us to marginalize, judge, pick on, and bully those who are different. Horror fans helped changed the rules by creating a forum where difference, creativity, weirdness, and otherness—being a monster kid—is celebrated. Horror fans have been my bravest companions on this road. I would never have found the Way of Being Lost if my horror fan heart tribe hadn't taught me how to lose my need to seem "normal" and helped me hoist my own freak flag. Horror fans have always known about the Way of Being Lost. I did, too— they just helped me remember that I was already on it.

Turns out, I have been a monster kid my whole life. I was just too busy hiding myself from myself to know it. In 2016, when I received the Monster Kid of the Year award, I was overjoyed. I proudly took my place among all the freaks and outcasts, iconoclasts and weirdoes— all of us who haven't felt like we fitted in, all of us who have felt like we were too different for our own good. All the monster kids of the world who are learning to embrace, enjoy, and celebrate who we are—and in so doing, shine our lights brightly into the world's darkness so that all the other spooky freaks and scary iconoclasts out there can find their way back home to their truest selves.

33

SOMEWHERE OVER THE RAINBOW

By acknowledging my inner monster kid and giving myself permission to let my freak flag fly, I reawakened maybe the most essential part of my truest self. When I began my spiritual journey in my twenties, I never would have guessed that this would be the key that unlocked the door to the life I had so long felt called to live. Although I grew up going to a loving church with *God is Love* emblazoned on our Sunday School wall, I also grew up with a fearful mother who believed that there was One Right Way to do everything—especially religion.

By the time I was a teenager, the difference between those two messages made me feel totally split. On the one hand, I trusted that Love just loved everyone. On the other hand, it seemed like I had to do all the right things to earn love—especially my mother's.

Although I had experienced the healing power of Love over and over again in my young life, I walked away from organized religion before I turned 20. I thought I would figure out my own way to love both myself and other people. That didn't go so well. By my mid-twenties, I felt utterly loveless. Religion hadn't worked, but neither had anything else I had tried. Something had to give.

The word that kept surfacing in my thoughts was "spirituality." What that meant to me was something more essential than religion. Something true that I could live from the inside out, instead of something moralistic dictated to me from the outside in.

I had grown up reading that heaven was within me—a place of pure peace, true good, and deep love. I also grew up believing that heaven was someplace we had to work hard to get to by being perfect. It seemed to me that the difference between those two heavens felt a lot like the difference between spirituality and religion. One felt like Love calling me back home. The other felt like fear trying to convince me that only by following its rules would I ever deserve the love I desired.

~

In 1987, when I was 25 years old, I came back to Los Angeles to be near my dying father. He and I had never had as much time together as I had wanted after he had married the woman who only somewhat jokingly called herself my wicked stepmother. Now, true to her snarky nickname, Coral made easy access to him almost impossible.

I was immensely grateful to be near him, but it wasn't always easy. I had returned to a hometown I hated in order to be near the person I loved most in the world, yet I was being kept away from him by someone who saw me, his own daughter, as a threat. On top of that, I was utterly unsure of who I was or what I wanted to do with my life.

The only lifeline I had was my desire to explore this new concept of spirituality.

One day during this time of intense confusion, I went for a hike in the hills above Los Angeles with my dear friends Bonnie and Diana and their friend Candace. I had never met Candace, but I had been hearing about how spiritual and intuitive she was. That description intrigued me. This was the late 1980s. People didn't throw those words around like they do now. There wasn't a yoga studio on every corner and a meditation workshop every weekend. The Internet didn't offer instant access to information about every spiritual tradition under the sun. Even the word "spirituality" felt foreign, which is why I had been really looking forward to our hike.

Candace seemed perfectly normal. The only thing about her that struck me were her piercingly blue eyes. But when we stopped in a beautiful field to take a break, Candace suddenly reached over, picked up my palm, and looked at it intently. Back then, however desperate I felt to find some comfort for my ontological angst, cynicism was my go-to response for most things that made me uncomfortable. The fact that I wasn't wisecracking as she gazed at my hand for what felt like an inordinately long time was a minor miracle. I realized how much I wanted her, needed her, to tell me something that would give me a sense of direction.

Eventually she began to speak. I don't remember anything she said except the one thing that I apparently needed to hear: "You have the ability to balance the physical, the intellectual, the emotional, and the spiritual. Most people don't have that. Right now what you are most neglecting is the spiritual."

Although my smart-aleck mind wanted to have a field day by judging her pronouncement as way too woo-woo, she had in fact put words to the void in my life. She not only had validated the emptiness I felt, but she had also given me the impetus to embrace a holistic idea of myself I had intuited but never had the courage to fully claim. I have never seen Candace since that afternoon, but I look back on that hike as the beginning of my spiritual journey.

After meeting Candace, I set my intention to find some kind of spiritual practice that could help me discover a measure of peace and wholeness. I just didn't know where to start. And let's face it, there are lots of other distractions when you're in your late twenties. I got caught up in most of them, but the calling just got louder and louder.

Gradually, my intense need for a lifeline reached a roaring crescendo. Doctors discovered my dad had Parkinson's. They put him on L-DOPA, and for a few years his quality of life improved. Then my stepmother died after a long battle with cancer. He was at once devastated and relieved; her illness had been immensely difficult and stressful on him. Soon, however, it was discovered he had cancer, too.

I spent a lot of time with my dad during his last years. Along with sharing meals and holidays and short excursions, three afternoons a week I drove up to his pink house perched above Sunset Boulevard and we worked on our book about his life and his lifelong passion for art. Watching my beloved father slowly die, I felt desperate for something to soothe my battered soul.

One rainy Saturday afternoon, I was stuck in my little apartment and my stress seemed to bounce right off the walls. I decided to draw a bath and soak while reading something I hoped would calm me. Although I was doing everything I could to try to stay centered, sometimes I just felt like it was all falling apart. I heard myself plead, almost desperately, "Please tell me where to start."

I got my answer. I heard back loud and clear: *Start with what you know.*

I went to my bookshelf and pulled out my old Sunday School books, got into the bath, and read: "To those leaning on the sustaining infinite, today is big with blessings." Aaaaahhhh! I leaned back into the warm water as I let those words reach deep into my heart, feeling, for the first time in over a decade, a deep peace wash over me. I felt hope and healing and promise. I felt Love. In that moment I reconnected with my fundamental belief that no matter what seems to be happening, there is something larger than all of us. That something larger I knew, I felt, I trusted, was Love.

Over the next few weeks, I read and read and read. The more I read, the more I really loved what I was reading—except for one major problem. I couldn't get past the word for that something larger: "God." Every time I read "God," I bumped smack up against some judgmental, authoritarian, moralistic patriarch who was ready and waiting to tell me all the ways I was a bad person. Although that wasn't what I fundamentally believed, that's how I felt.

Then I read something else that shifted everything. I read that the word for "God" and the word for "good" were exactly the same word in many languages. So I decided to just substitute "Good" for "God." Every time I read "God," I thought "Good." Good is Love. Good is All-in-all. Good is my Higher Power. Good is omnipotent.

Did I believe that? Did I believe that Good is everything, all powerful, everyone? Yes, with my whole heart. Even now, I use whatever word for that larger good that feels true in the moment: Source, Spirit, Life, Truth, Love, Mind, or God. They are all Good.

We are all born believing in that greater good, which manifests when we are babies as loving and trusting our own and everyone else's goodness. As we grow up and begin to listen to the world more than we listen to our own hearts, however, that natural expectation of good begins to seem less and less real. Without that foundational love-based belief, we build our lives on the quicksand of fear. This inevitably entraps us in lack. Lack of money or love or intelligence or happiness or health. From that place of scarcity, nothing is ever enough. Eventually we settle for "not so bad." Not enough and not so bad are a far, far cry from the bedrock of Love we once trusted.

When we lose the natural expectation of good, we begin to believe that evil is more powerful than good. We have clouded over the beautiful reality of good by viewing our lives through the warped looking glass of fear.

In my twenties, I was very active in the anti-nuclear movement. Over time, I became so scared that the whole world was going to be blown up that it practically paralyzed me with fear. One day I revealed my fears to my older brother Barrett, who shared something with such kindness that I heard it deeply and never forgot it.

"Do you know what Gandhi believed?" he asked me. "All the violence in the world, all the Hitlers and Holocausts, will never have the power to outweigh the simple daily acts of good." When he said that, I felt the truth behind his words. In that moment, I literally *felt* the millions of daily expressions of kindness happening even as we sat there in that diner booth together. In my mind's eye I saw all the helping hands and hugs and sympathetic ears. I knew in my heart that Gandhi and my brother were right: The hundreds of thousands of those moments of goodness every day could never be nuked into oblivion.

When we delve beneath our tendency to cling to fear and let Love slide off of us, we recognize that, despite our temptation to rubberneck our way through the world transfixed by every terrible thing we watch on the news, our hearts never stop expecting good. We just have to remember to listen to our hearts instead of our heads.

That can feel so hard sometimes. We often end up arguing more stridently for limitation and lack than we do for deservability and self-worth. As if that weren't enough, we give that denigrating attitude a virtuous name. We call it humility. We've got that rhyme all wrong. Humility is *not* unworthiness or lack of deservability.

When I found this passage in *A Course in Miracles*, it shone off the page and into my heart: "You are the light of the world . . . This is merely a statement of the truth about yourself. It is the opposite of a statement of pride, of arrogance, or of self-deception . . . It refers to you as you were created by God. True humility requires that you accept this idea because it is God's Voice which tells you it is true. This is a beginning step in accepting your real function on earth."

One of my deepest desires in exploring spirituality had been to find my "real function on earth." Like most people in their twenties, I had been trying everything to discover who I was meant to be and what I was here to do in the world. But the more I tried to "be" something—I went to graduate school to get advanced degrees, I took prestigious jobs in glamorous fields—the further and further away I felt from myself. When I read that passage in *A Course in Miracles*, however, everything shifted. All I had to do, I realized, was to learn how to shine my light. Everything else would follow.

From that moment on, my spiritual practice became the mainstay of my life. I never wavered in getting up an hour or two early every morning to pray, read, and journal. I began each day with my childhood prayer connecting me to my Divine Source: *Be glad, give thanks, rejoice.* I came to think of God as the Sun—and all of us as God's rays here to shine. I loved that metaphor, because the sun and its rays aren't two separate things. The sun isn't the sun if it doesn't have its rays to spread its warmth and light, while those rays just naturally emanate that warmth and light of the sun. In other words, the sun and its rays are one.

The rays don't have to try to shine their light. They don't wonder what to *do* to shine better or more brightly. They don't worry that they don't have what it takes to shine. They don't quibble with one another—*Gosh, you get to shine on the Hollywood sign, while I'm stuck over here trying to break through all these clouds above the North Pole.* They aren't competitive or jealous: *How come you get to shine on Benedict Cumberbatch and I got stuck with this disgusting dumpster?* They most certainly don't say, *I really don't deserve to be a ray. Maybe you should pick someone else. I'm not light enough, bright enough, or warm enough.*

False humility would have us believe we're not good enough or we need to do something more to be good enough. None of us has to do anything more or better or righter to be any more connected than we already are to our Source. We are all rays and we are all here to shine. It's what we do naturally.

There was only one problem in my dedicated spiritual practice. Although I understood these beautiful ideas in my head, they were so much harder to believe in my heart. It seemed far easier to listen to my false self convince me that there was something I had to do, or do better, in order to shine. Fear often clouded my light. The good news was—my light didn't go anywhere. I caught glimpses of my light when I was traveling or spending time with my dogs or doing creative work. But it wasn't until I began practicing joy that I truly began to shine. Then, as I began to hear the voice of my true self, I heard something else I had tried to tune out for decades. Something I needed to remember if I was ever going to be able to show up in the world as I longed to do.

I have always felt the calling of Spirit. Even as a little girl, when I first read about the lives of monks who lived and prayed and studied—and trained dogs or grew vegetables—in monasteries, my whole being ached to be one of them.

On a trip to Portugal when I was in my early thirties, I stayed in a historic inn that had once been a monastery. My room had been a monk's cell. Every morning when I got up to write in my spiritual journal, I sat in the deep stone window seat that looked over the gardens. I could feel the indentation created by all the monks who had sat there and prayed for hundreds of years before me. It was powerful.

However . . . I was not male, nor did I belong to (or wish to belong to) any kind of religious order. Logically, wanting to be a monk made absolutely no sense. So I never did anything about this deep monastic longing for spiritual community and connection. I just continued along my isolated spiritual path.

After I began my joy practice, however, I realized that I could no longer ignore my desire for spiritual connection and community. Although I felt scared to share my mystical metaphysical approach to life and love with others, I also knew that I could not really live my practice of joy if I did not step out of my spiritual closet. But that felt terrifying. I was afraid of being judged, mocked, and ridiculed for my outside-the-box spiritual beliefs. Yet I had no other choice.

Most of us are terrified to let ourselves be seen naked and vulnerable and true. We would much rather hide than show our hearts to one another. To begin to write and live myself whole, I realized that I had to be willing to share both the heart of my spiritual seeking and the heart that has screwed up over and over again. I had to be willing to let other people see not only the bone-headed, reprehensible, irresponsible, questionable, and sometimes even mean things I have done, but also all the spiritual hopes and aspirations I have always held. Because if I don't tell the truth, I can't live it.

254

To do this, I had to open my heart in a brand-new way—I needed a spiritual community. I just didn't know where to start looking for it. I had tried traditional churches, but I always felt a far greater connection to the Divine when I hiked in nature with my dogs. I looked into seminaries and grad schools, but they all seemed too academic and far too expensive.

Until one afternoon in 2012, feeling particularly freaked out about all the changes I had been making while trying to show up to my own life, I drew a bath in the middle of the afternoon. I reached for a spiritual magazine that a friend had given me. That's when an ad for an interfaith/interspiritual seminary caught my eye.

I knew that interfaith honors and acknowledges all religious traditions, but I'd never heard of interspirituality. When I read that interspirituality embraces and integrates all spiritual paths, including nature, animals, poetry, joy, laughter, ritual, and so much more, I felt like I had come home. That's how I'd always moved through the world. To study to become a minister of this integral approach, which encompasses both service and individual experience as it relates to our planet as a whole, felt like a dream come true.

I have felt interspiritual my whole life. I had just been trying to wildflower in the disturbed soil between traditional religion and a more holistic spirituality all by myself.

I found out that this was a mostly online program and that the cost was reasonable, so I applied—and was accepted. I was elated!

The first tradition we studied in seminary was Hinduism. Hinduism believes that all spiritual paths lead to the same goal, and that to claim salvation as the monopoly of one belies the whole nature of the Universe. When I read this quote by Ramakrishna, I almost cried: "As a mother, in nursing her sick children, gives rice and curry to one, and sago arrowroot to another, and bread and butter to a third, so the Lord has laid out different paths for different people suitable for their natures."

Up to that point in my spiritual life, I had never quite been able to shake my fear of deviating from my mother's One Right Way. Now I was reading what I had always known in my heart—there are many paths to All Good. During that first year, I was overjoyed by the beauty, hope, and connection I saw through the diverse religious and spiritual paths we studied. I loved what I was learning—and all the ways it made sense. Toward the end of my first year, however, I hit the roadblock of a huge realization: Although I had really been enjoying my studies, I hadn't created any kind of community. I had come to seminary with the dream of connecting through my own heart to the hearts of others, but my heart had remained closed.

Knowing that I wasn't experiencing the program in the way that I needed to, I dropped out of seminary just two weeks before the required final intensive. My dean thought I was crazy, but I knew what I had to do. I had to get off some superficial superhighway to spirituality and recommit to the interspiritual beauty of my heart-based back roads. I couldn't create community if I didn't know where to find my own heart. To do that, I had to reconnect with joy. Once I did, I re-enrolled.

It's no coincidence that I rejoined seminary just as I began to create my daily practice of joy. From the very first day with my new classmates, I knew I had found my spiritual heart tribe.

Although I was studying the same things I had already learned all over again, I experienced everything in a completely different way this time. For the next two years, my heart was cracked open over and over again by my fellow seminarians, who showed up to every class, every experience, and every interaction with such immense love, humility, and kindness that they illumined the path I knew I wanted to take: the Path of Love.

Sometimes the hardest thing to do on the Way of Being Lost is to lose your idea of what you're supposed to be doing there. In my first go at my first year, I had never gotten out of my own head. When I re-entered seminary, instead of using my brain to memorize facts the way I had the first time, I learned to *feel* the concepts in my heart. To see from our hearts is to connect with one another's spirits.

I felt so embraced by my new classmates that, for the first time in my life, I was willing to begin sharing my spiritual beliefs with others. Along with everything else my mother asked me to hide, she taught me never to talk about religion. Religion, she believed, was something private and sacred that you didn't talk about in public. So I never did.

When I grew up and came out, the condemnation of the LBGTQ community by almost every major religion made me feel like there was no place I could be honest and still be a part of a mainstream religion. The few times I risked sharing my spiritual journey with others, I often felt lonelier than when I kept my practice to myself. To risk sharing what was most precious to me and to feel judged or misunderstood felt devastating.

Eventually I came to realize that having been a spiritual outsider for all those years had actually been a gift. It had given me both a compassionate perspective and an inner strength that has kept me going in the darkest times of my life.

When I discovered interspirituality, I realized that there were a lot more people like me than I had ever imagined. Finding my heart tribe taught me the healing power of loving acceptance and support. They helped me come out of my spiritual closet in the most healing and hopeful ways.

Then I just kept coming out . . .

34

WHY, OH WHY, CAN'T I?

In June 2015, I flew to New York to attend our first required intensive. It turned out to be one of the most extraordinary weeks of my life. This was the first time I met my heart tribe face to face. Here were 75 people who instantly felt like my soulmates. For the first time since beginning my daily practice of joy, I didn't have to remember to practice joy. I just lived it! In the presence of this group of cracked-open hearts, I understood something for the first time: We can only truly experience love when we feel completely safe.

On the last day of our intensive, Reverend Joyce, the associate director of our seminary, stood up to speak to our class. She was a diminutive, white-haired woman who looked like a nonsectarian nun. She had spoken little during the four days, but when she did, it was with a twinkle in her eye and the authority of a Biblical scholar.

She told the story of taking a workshop in New York City during the 1970s, at the end of which the moderator invited all the gays and lesbians to come to the front of the room. Reverend Joyce had been frightened because gays and lesbians could be arrested in those days. But up to the front she went. Then the moderator did something that she never forgot.

"She asked the audience to applaud," Reverend Joyce remembered, "saying that 'acknowledgement was a profound form of loving. Perhaps the greatest form of loving.' There was great applause and cheerful yelling and clapping. It was a profound moment in my life. I was and continue to be so very grateful to her for doing this."

When Reverend Joyce finished sharing this story, she looked at all of us and then invited everyone who identified anywhere on the rainbow spectrum to stand up in front of the rest of the class. She named everything she could think of from that spectrum—letters I hadn't even considered. One of the names she spoke was "two spirit."

I first heard about the Native American concept of two spirit in graduate school in the mid-1980s while reading a book about how a Zuni *berdache*—a man who had lived as a woman—had been deeply revered for his spiritual power and leadership abilities and had even met the president of the United States as a representative of his tribe. Although the book was fascinating, nothing about the idea of being two spirit called to me personally at that time. But when I heard the term thirty years later in a completely new context, it resonated in my heart.

So much had changed in the world since I was in my twenties. New generations of brave young people were finding the courage to speak their truths and to create new ideas of love and partnership, gender and sexuality, commitment and connection, which were so much more fluid than any previous generation had believed possible.

As I got to know some of these young people, I realized their coming out was not really about sexuality as much as it was about redefining gender and the freedom to love—both for themselves and for others. Getting to know trans teenagers, who understood that they had been put in the wrong body and who were fighting to be seen for who they knew themselves to be inside, had a particularly profound impact on me. Their incredible courage to name themselves when the adult world refused to believe them blew my mind. Their understanding that if they were not true to themselves, then there was no way they could be true to the world, became a huge part of my own healing journey. It took witnessing this courage of a younger generation to begin to allow myself the permission to begin to define myself.

When Reverend Joyce spoke the words "two spirit," something clicked. In that moment, I recognized that *I* was two spirit, though I didn't yet know what exactly that meant.

With about fifteen other people, both students and deans, I stood up as Reverend Joyce had done forty years earlier and went to the front of the room. Then she asked the rest of the class to applaud, affirm, and acknowledge us. Everyone else in the room stood up and cheered and applauded and loved us all up big time. Standing up there, I cried like a baby.

I had been publicly "out" as a lesbian for decades, yet I had never felt like a lesbian. When I heard the words "two spirit," I stood up for the first time as my true self. I had come home to my own heart.

In the months after the intensive, I began to understand that my true self identifies as spiritual rather than sexual. I am drawn to others through a soul connection that may or may not include physical attraction—but even when I am attracted to someone, sex is the least important thing to me. Because I had never understood that about myself, I had never been able to express that to anyone else. That was why so many of my relationships failed. I had never shown up as my true self. It wasn't until I acknowledged my spiritual calling and felt embraced by my spiritual heart tribe that all the pieces in this puzzle of me finally began to fit.

For as long as I can remember, I have felt twinned inside myself as both male and female. Not male and female in terms of physical or biological identity. I identify as two spirit because I feel that my true self manifests beyond our physical or sexual ideas of male or female—even beyond gender identity.

I believe that as spiritual beings, we ultimately encompass and express all supposedly gender-based qualities. It is only society and the material world that seeks to identify us physically or sexually, to label us and put us in boxes. We all express the divine masculine and feminine. I had felt this even—maybe especially—as a little girl. But never having seen it articulated by anyone else, I felt crazy. So I hid that essential me not just from the outside world, but even from myself.

For now, two spirit is the closest term I have for my true self. Having many Native American friends, I recognize that my understanding of two spirit is precisely that—*my* understanding. All we can know about any idea amounts to our understanding of it.

For me, identifying as two spirit meant that after years of trying to be someone I'm not—for my parents, for churches and religion, for my family legacy, for the gay community, for myself—for the first time I felt able to show up in the world true. To do that, however, I not only had to be willing to lose everyone else's false ideas about me. I also had to get rid of a few of my own. I had to forgive myself for all the ways I felt that I had failed others—especially in love. I realized that, although I had genuinely tried my best in every relationship, I had never shown up as who I was. I had put so much effort into trying to be someone I never was, instead of showing up in truth. I had been unable to show up as my best self, because I never let myself acknowledge who she really was. In order to learn how to love as my true two-spirit self, I had to keep discovering who I really am.

I learned this in the most beautiful of ways on a Sunday afternoon while bird-watching with a friend. After sighting a few mature Indigo Buntings, as well as a number of smaller, equally bright blue birds, I put voice to something I had been wondering: "I know the bigger blue birds are the Indigo Buntings, but when I look in the books for the smaller bright blue ones, I can't find them." As I said it, I felt that old junior high feeling that there was something I "should" know but didn't. So I felt junior high school relief when my friend said she didn't know either. We speculated together as to whether they were immature birds, new nestlings just learning to fly and sing. We ended up being very comfortable in our not knowing.

263

It was then that she said: "I once read that if the bird you see doesn't match the picture or the description of the bird in the books, the bird is always right."

I looked at her and a huge grin broke out on my face, mirrored back by an equally big one on hers. Of course! How sweet and how true! What a perfect metaphor for, well, everything . . .

The bird is always right!

My whole life, I've felt as though I have been asked to check some box that was supposed to represent me. But none of the boxes ever seem to match how I see myself. None of the boxes, none of the labels, none of the initials or titles have ever felt like me.

We've all been asked to tick some box that is supposed to describe us. We've all been taught that we are different but the same, separate but united. Yet under every skin color; every uniform; every political affiliation; every sexual orientation or gender identification; every nationality, religion, or ethnicity; every body size; every ability or seeming disability, I believe there is an individual at least part of whom has never felt as though there were a box to check, an initial to choose, a profession to pick, a lifestyle to live that fully fit who they felt themselves to be. In one way or another, all of us have wondered at one time or another in our lives why the descriptions in the book didn't match the plumage that we feel.

Even when I was a kid, my mother never quite knew what to make of me. Sometimes I would come down to breakfast wearing an outfit she thought so misguided—oh, let's say, a Japanese kimono with a cowboy hat and leg warmers over my pastel-colored school uniform—and her whole face would blanch. "What kind of a statement are you trying to make with *that*?" she would ask, horrified.

I always felt as if I had to give her an answer—but my answers really never made any sense because what I wanted to say was simply, "This is the me I felt like being today. "

At some point, when she had heard enough, she always trotted out her old adage: "Well, unless you're going to have a T-shirt printed explaining all of that—and what you just said is going to take up the whole front and back—no one is going to know what you mean. You don't want to go through life having to explain yourself to everyone, do you?"

Well, no. I didn't. I didn't see why I had to, really. So what if I was a kimono-cowboy-hat-leg-warmer-wearing tall white girl who didn't really want to be white at all? What did that matter? Apparently it did to my mother—and a lot of people like her. I have spent far too much of my life trying to fit into the box I never felt but that I nonetheless checked on a census form whose import was lost on me, choosing a major that covered only a minor amount of my interests, attempting to get comfortable being an initial that never matched my heart, identifying as sexual when what I felt was spiritual, and reducing the weird array of me to a clever T-shirt slogan that everyone could "get."

It hasn't worked.

The longer I am alive, the more I think every single person on the planet occupies their own uniquely unlabelable-whole-alphabet-I-had-to-pick-something-but-this-box-doesn't-even-come-close reality. Eventually, we all will discover that this is the only address accepting mail on the Way of Being Lost.

That Sunday morning, as I wondered why I couldn't find the little blue birds I saw in the field in any of my books, feeling confused, even wrong, suddenly it seemed so obvious—actually so wonderfully funny—to think that any of us humans could presume to know, to even want to label, the beauty of those little blue birds. *Who cared what they were called?* All I wanted to do was to enjoy them—to listen to their sweet trilling songs, watch them flit across the fields, see the sun glint off their blue feathers. I wanted to be with them and love them—be they buntings or bluebirds or something else altogether.

If it's hard for us to do with birds—to resist the taxonomies that we use to wrangle the wild into submission—no wonder we can't do it with ourselves. Let alone with one another. Only when we are willing to lose our compulsion to categorize can we revel in the wonderful wilderness of unknowing that is the Way of Being Lost.

The solution to our fears is not to squeeze ourselves inside the box, any more than the "best" way to travel is the most direct route. The answer to our dilemma is not to pick a letter of the alphabet and try to live it with as little misery as possible. The healing of the world is never going to be creating more labels that reduce everything to more meaningless iterations of us and them. We must try to resist the need to comfort ourselves with labels, and instead choose Love. When we choose Love, we live Love. When we choose Love, us and them just dissolves into One.

⌒

On the Way of Being Lost, I have had to learn to find my bearings neither where I hoped to be nor as who I thought I was. That means learning to love myself right where I am. I used to wish that I was "like everyone else." Now I recognize that nonconformity—in school, religion, celebrity, sexuality, creativity, home, and relationships—has been one of the greatest gifts of my life. It is the disturbed soil in which I have learned to wildflower myself whole.

My whole life I had wondered why, oh why, can't I live and love like other people seem to be able to do.

By losing all the labels, I finally was able to choose Love and find my heart tribes.

When we choose Love, we *can* fly over the rainbow.

When we choose Love, the bird *is* always right.

35

SURRENDER, DOROTHY

Sometimes, however, when we choose Love everything seems to go to hell in Toto's handbasket.

In my last semester of seminary, every part of my life seemed to present me with a test I could not seem to pass—and in all of my most difficult subjects: love, money, belonging, spirituality, worthiness, and home. I had worked so hard and come so far, only to find myself blitzkrieged by what felt like every conceivable fear:

Would I ever truly believe I was worthy of love?

Would I ever find financial ease?

Would I ever stop working myself to the bone?

Would I ever feel like what I did gave back something to the world?

I couldn't understand why things seemed to be getting harder instead of easier. I was creating a daily practice of joy and facing down all the old voices of my joy kills. I had found heart tribes in the horror community and in my seminary class. I had come out of the spiritual closet and embraced my two-spiritedness. Now I was about to be ordained as an interspiritual minister. But instead of flying over the rainbow with my new friends, my joy was being abducted by the flying monkeys of my fears. So where was my Technicolor happy ending? Frankly, I would have welcomed a field of poppies to put me to sleep. Anything to stop this spiraling anxiety.

Here I was—finally spiritually awake and alive in joy—yet longing to go back to sleep!

That was my lightbulb moment—allowing me to finally recognize perhaps the most deeply grooved pattern of my life: When push comes to shove, I tend to toss my spiritual promises to myself out the window. Praying and surrendering and letting go is all well and good on a nice sunny day reading a romance novel on the beach. But when it feels like the world is falling apart all around me? Not so much.

My whole life I had talked a good game about the importance of spiritual practice. But practice is only practice if you practice it every day. That final semester of seminary, as my angst ratcheted up, I had stopped being willing to be crumbled and surrender, to learn and listen, to pray.

All of my angst was being called out onto the carpet and into the light of day because Love was stirring all my old fears up in order to dismantle them. I realized I was being asked to find a new way.

⌒

When I was a teenager, I confidently told my friends: *I'm going to be a late bloomer. I'm one of those people who is going to get better with age.* But in my twenties, as I watched everyone I knew blossom into forsythia and daffodils, lilacs and peonies, being a late bloomer didn't seem like such a great idea. I thought something was really wrong with me for not blossoming into love and creativity and joy. The seasons changed; spring then summer came and went. I began to wonder: Would I ever bloom?

I could feel my own autumn in the air that spring of 2011 when, as Anaïs Nin foretold, "the day came when the risk to remain tight in a bud was more painful than the risk it took to bloom." Then I had to learn to fertilize my disturbed soil with joy in order to risk opening my heart and wildflowering. After that, no matter the droughts or the deluges in my life, I refused to wither. But that final semester in seminary, I seriously doubted my own resolve.

That winter I had been working on a design project that I loved in Austin. Nonetheless, after two months of living in a dusty, loud construction site, all I felt was stressed and exhausted. Even my creative work and my very environment seemed to be testing me. I began to wonder how much more I could withstand.

The weather outside mirrored my internal barometer. Every day leaden grey skies released tempestuous squalls of sideways rain. Whenever it stopped, I walked the Austin hills. That's when I began to notice tiny, tightly curled, deep purple buds poking their heads up from clumps of new green grass. The famous Texas bluebonnets were getting ready to bloom.

Then one day, it just happened. The Hill Country erupted into gorgeous multicolored blankets of bluebonnets and bright orange paintbrush and yellow-and-red blanket flowers. Every hill wildflowered into a rainbow of colors.

After weeks of stormy doubt, it was as if the whole Universe had conspired to broadcast exactly what I needed to hear: You are ready to bloom!

A few days later, I stumbled across this fragment of a poem by the fourteenth-century Sufi poet Rumi:

Be crumbled,

so wildflowers will come up

where you are.

> *You've been stony for too many years.*

Try something different.

Surrender.

From the depths of perhaps my darkest night of the soul, I felt as though I had been gifted across the centuries with my own instruction manual for wildflowering into the Way of Being Lost.

Step One: Be Crumbled

We live in a society that celebrates success, where we learn to hide our shameful secrets and our shadows. We submerge them in our subconscious, hoping that they are gone for good. They aren't. They always resurface. The swamp things of our lives will always bubble up from the festering deep.

Here's what we have to remember: When these swamp monsters finally do emerge, it is actually Truth uncovering the toxins we need to expel—no matter how unpleasant it may feel. This is the Truth that sets us free. By bringing our darkest stories out into the light, Truth helps us see that they were never really true anyway.

It's hard to step out of the comfort zones of our false selves, but that's why we have to be willing to be crumbled. Nothing can grow in impacted soil. Only where the soil of our lives is disturbed, crumbled by the collision between fear and love, hate and kindness, joy and sorrow, can we begin to wildflower. That's why our greatest teachings will always come from facing down our fears. Only when we crumble can we bloom.

Step Two: Let Wildflowers Come Up

The fear whispering in our ear doesn't want us to wildflower because wildflowers do everything fear has taught us to avoid. Wildflowers are free! They seed themselves wherever the wind takes them. They grow in every color, shape, and size. They are not cultivated, orderly, or tended. Weeds can be wildflowers, and wildflowers can be weeds. You can't tell the difference, and no one cares.

As anyone who has reveled in a field of wildflowers knows, the more there are, the more beautiful the field. Fear doesn't like that. Fear avoids connection. It uses isolation to do its dirty work. When we wildflower, we come together in our collective beauty, grace, and power. We come together in Love.

Eventually, of course, spring ends and the wildflowers fade away. Summer comes and seeds scatter. Fall comes disturbing the soil. Winter rains water that soil. But come spring, the wildflowers bloom again—because that's what wildflowers do.

Step Three: Leave Stoniness Behind

As we learn to let ourselves wildflower, we begin to reject the stoniness of fear. To do that, however, goes against so much of what we are taught. We are taught that rock is a firm foundation and that stoniness is safe. Growing up in Los Angeles, I learned that the place you want to be when The Big One hits is on the bedrock. Religion tells us the same thing: Don't build your houses on sand. Choose

273

the firm foundation of religious rock. But for many of us who have felt excluded and rejected by the rigid views of traditional religion, that Rock has been anything but safe. Consequently we have felt called to leave behind the stones that build the walls that separate, the stones that entomb, the stones that are too often thrown.

As we learn to bloom in our disturbed soil, we evolve like wildflowers—into new species, hybrids, and colors, letting the wind and bees take our seeds where they will. In doing so, wildflowers are not just surviving, but truly deeply thriving.

Step Four: Try Something Different

To leave behind the stony safety that our false selves crave can feel terrifying. The same old, same old may feel boring at times, but at least it feels safe because you always know what to expect and the rug is never yanked out from underneath you.

Implicit in the comforting belief of the One Right Way, however, is the condemnation of many, many "wrong" ways. If there can only be one right, all difference becomes wrong, bad, and scary. It's Us = good, safe, right. Them = bad, scary, wrong. We are educated to believe that some people are better than, smarter than, more successful than, prettier than, or happier than others. Whichever side of that comparative "than" we're on, we both judge and fear the other.

At the end of the day, those dualities always fail to bring us our longed-for security. The moment we start trying to promote, protect, and preserve our own individual little kingdoms, fear has us right where it wants us. We become afraid we will lose or fail because someone else might be better, smarter, more successful, prettier, or happier than we are!

In truth, healing comes only by embracing difference, individuality, choice, and creativity in all its myriad forms—and then recognizing that all those different threads and textures and colors and shapes and sizes actually form a giant tapestry of Love.

The only way we can ever feel safe is to know we are all One.

Step Five: Surrender

A gun in the back. The Wicked Witch writing a giant threat in the sky on her broom. Waving the white flag. Surrender is a word connoting so many things.

At the end of a war, it is usually the superior officers who do the actual surrendering. This means that when the foot soldiers get word of the armistice, they are told to lay their weapons down wherever they are and sit by the side of the road to await further instruction.

Every day, we have to lay down whatever weapons we have carried into conflict—like judgment, anger, and hatred—and be willing to sit by the side of the road and await further instruction from our supreme Superior Officer.

Hope, wholeness, and healing always come when we are willing to surrender.

Father Richard Rohr tells this amazing story: After World War II ended in the Pacific Theatre, there were many tiny islands occupied by Japanese soldiers who, for years, did not know that the war was over. By the time these soldiers were discovered and brought home, some of them had been on their isolated outposts for a very long time. They found it extremely difficult to reintegrate into the lives of their villages, which made daily life challenging for everyone. So the villagers created a ritual for these loyal soldiers.

Everyone in the village gathered together around the soldier, and one by one they reflected back to that solider all the ways in which he had served their country and upheld their honor. One by one they thanked him for his service and for expressing each of these qualities that had made him an incredible soldier *but did not have a place in everyday life.* One by one they told him that he could release those qualities because they were no longer needed. They assured him that he would always be able to call on those same qualities were they ever needed again, but for now they could be gratefully and peacefully set aside.

We all need help learning to release qualities that may once have served us but no longer do. The ways in which we learned to be responsible, moral, ethical, and disciplined when we were younger may keep us stuck as limiting dualities that make us feel separate, superior, or special in the world. We can thank those qualities for their service to us and then lay them aside, with the assurance that they will always be there if we need them again.

Surrendering is an ongoing cycle. Each of us has to find our own way to wildflower. When we do, we seed the whole world. By being willing to release anything that no longer serves us, even if we don't know what will replace it, we inevitably discover the heart of who we have always known ourselves to be. We remember our truest selves.

Right there, in the disturbed soil between an old way of being and new way of seeing, we stand on the threshold of a new life. Instead of fighting or fleeing our differences, we learn to hold the creative tension between deeply entrenched dualities. We depart from the stony binary world of separation and so enter a new multidimensional world of reconciliation. We wildflower in the field that Rumi knew existed beyond all our learned ideas of wrongdoing and rightdoing: the Unified Field of Love where we can blossom whole together.

Surrounded by the beauty of the wildflowering Texas hills and guided by Rumi, I had been shown my path. It was time for me to blossom right there in the disturbed soil of this darkest night of my soul.

36

MY
RED SHOES

In the wee hours of the morning of that spring equinox, I woke up bolt upright and couldn't fall back to sleep. I made the mistake of checking my emails. There was one from my landlord in Santa Fe telling me that he needed to sell my wonderful home of the past two and a half years and that I had to be out in two months. Sleep never came again that night in Austin, as panic filled my chest.

Making this already stressful news even more stressful, I was scheduled to be home for only three weeks over that two-month period due to design work, speaking engagements and convention appearances. On top of all that, I was up for jury duty.

"What," I asked the Universe, "do you want me to learn *now*?"

The answer came through loud and clear: Lean, trust, and ask for help.

For those of us who have been brought up to believe that it is our job to be self-sufficient, to never show weakness, to never count on anyone for anything, asking for help can sometimes feel scarier than continuing to suffer. Yet often the greatest gift of our lives is being brought to a place where we know we cannot move forward alone anymore.

On my knees, I asked for help.

Help came—in the form of loving emails, words of wisdom from the Universe, and even a few seeming miracles.

The senior dean of the second-year students at my seminary sent me a short email out of the blue, which said exactly what I needed to remember: "God is everywhere present. God is in this and I understand why you would feel that you have to turn away to find God, but God is right there."

That stopped me in my tracks. I had lost sight of the one thing I always said was most important to me: Seeing God right where I was—in the problems, the fears, the messiness of my life.

The next afternoon, after ten straight days of rain the clouds finally lifted. I decided to head out for a long hike by the river in the sunshine—only to find myself slipping and sliding along the banks. That hike felt like my life—unstable, unsafe, and dangerously slippery.

Praying as I negotiated the unreliable trail, I asked to be given some answers to all the hard questions of my life, and to trust that I really was ready to bloom.

These words came to me: "Hold the contradictions."

Huh? What did that mean?

I heard it again.

"Hold the contradictions."

I knew that this was my answer.

⌒

Over the next few days, I realized that I was being called to take a pretty radical step. I'd been living on the road for over

200 nights a year for a couple of years—between design work, speaking engagements, and appearances. Although I loved many aspects of my work as a designer, increasingly I felt called to find a way to make my living doing something that gave back to the world. I wanted to commit to creating a life of inspirational speaking, writing, and workshops. But that would mean pulling back from the work that had been paying my bills in order to risk a new and very uncertain way of living. To do that without the safety net of money felt crazy. But this time, the Universe had made it abundantly clear that turning back was not an option.

I realized that I was being asked to surrender the idea of living in one place for a while, and follow the yellow brick road of my dream. That felt both scary and exciting.

What didn't feel good at all was the realization that I had to find a safe, stable home for my beloved 15-year-old Dalmatian, Jack, who was now too old to join me on my journey.

I had met a wonderful South African woman who was staying with him when I traveled. They loved one another, so as long as I could give her a place to stay, Jack had a surrogate mom. Without a house, however, neither of them would have a home.

I knew what I had to do, but knowing what you have to do and finding the courage to do it are two different things. My stress level, which was already high, went off the charts once I realized that I was going to have to let go of my beautiful boy. I began praying, surrendering, holding the contradictions, and leaning on the Divine.

After an anxious week of letting go and leaning, praying, loving, and trusting, I got the nudge to call the lovely couple from Albuquerque who had originally rescued and fostered Jack 14 years earlier, hand nursing him back to health after he was mauled almost to death by wild dogs. I knew they no longer rescued and fostered dogs, but they remembered both me and Jack—and they immediately invited my beautiful boy back into their home. There were no words to describe the relief and joy and gratitude I felt— both for them and for the proof that Love always takes us full circle.

For the next nine months, Elaine and Marc Price (yes, we have the same last name!) cared for Jack, giving him a wonderful life and home until together, we made the decision that it was time to let him go Home.

Once again, I had been given the help I needed.

On my drive back to Santa Fe from Austin to pack up my house and say goodbye to Jack, I kept hearing another sentence over and over again:

Let it all go.

What the hell, I thought. *I'm already letting go of my home and my dog. Isn't that enough already?*

So I didn't listen. Instead I decided to look for an apartment that could serve as storage unit-cum-flop pad. After I had looked at a few places, the message bullhorned again: *Let it all go.*

OK, I figured. I'll just store everything for a few months and figure it all out later. Then I did the math. I couldn't afford to store everything I owned.

Now what?

Oh right.

Let it all go.

⁓

And that's how I became intentionally homeless.

On May 15, 2016, less than two months after receiving my

landlord's email, I stood outside my doorway in a new pair of red sneakers—my own ruby slippers to accompany me down the yellow brick road of intentional homelessness that lay before me. I said goodbye to Santa Fe, the town I'd called home for a quarter century, and I began my walkabout.

I was joined by my very own Toto—a small, white, fluffy doodle puppy named Allie, who had unexpectedly come into my life to be my brave companion on the road. As the Bodhisattva Love Mayor of the World, she has turned out to be supremely suited for this job. I left without knowing where I would go, how long it would take, or whom I would meet along the way.

Being lost, living on the road without a home base, is what I have been called to do. It may sound glamorous. It may sound like freedom. In part, it is. It's also lonely and scary—not knowing where you're going to sleep, wondering how you're going to pay the bills, and questioning whether the whole idea was just plain pathological in the first place.

But I'll say this—it *is* always revelatory. Unlike "real life," on the road you *want* to leave your crap behind, and the goal (if there even is one) is never the *where*, but always the *how*. Whenever we discard our junk and show up to that how instead of to the where, the what, or the why, we discover The Way.

Before I became intentionally homeless, I believed that life was a process of accumulation, accretion, and accrual. I layered experience upon experience, belief upon belief, story upon story. I larded life on, year after year, padding and weighing myself down with all the mental, physical, psychological, and emotional stuff I thought made me "me."

On the Way of Being Lost, I learned that we have to be willing to leave behind the ego container of our false selves—the identities we accrue through education, family, career, money, clothing, resumes, and even religion—so that we can return to the true self who is waiting for each of us to come home. To lose what we have spent our whole lives trying to find: power, prestige, potential, and possessions.

⌒

Toward the end of my mother's life, she struggled with many issues—physical illness as well as a heart that had grown so hard that it argued against even the things and the people who had brought her the most joy and healing. A few years before she died, a woman who knew her well and loved her deeply said, "I feel that there is a word you need to think about, my dear. The word is accumulation."

When my mother shared that with me, I knew her friend was right. I could feel it. I wasn't sure what she needed to do about it, but I knew in my gut that accumulation was at the heart of all of her issues. What I didn't know is that it was also at the heart of all of mine.

After my mother's death in 2002, it had fallen to me to clear out her three houses and fifteen storage units in Boston, Santa Fe, Los Angeles, and Honolulu. I had never seen so much stuff in my life. *Wow!* I thought. *Thank goodness I'm not like her.*

A few years later, I decided that it was time for me to move. I asked a friend to help me sort out what I wanted to keep and what I wanted to toss, because I felt so overwhelmed by the task. She and I worked together in the house for hours. We were knee-deep in my shoes when she turned to me and quietly said, "You know, if I had this much stuff, I'd be overwhelmed, too."

I honestly hadn't seen that I was just like my mother. Accumulation, accrual, and accretion—that's what I had been raised to do so unconsciously that it felt to me like breathing.

When I committed to a life of intentional homelessness, I went through every single thing I owned deciding whether or not to keep it. I held each object in my hand and let myself feel whether or not it sparked joy. Whatever did not, I released.

By being willing to slag my accumulated small selves in exchange for the prospect of the pure gold of my true self, by releasing the idea of a conventional home and so much of what I had thought I was supposed to accumulate, I also released a lifetime of outside expectations and aspirations. In doing that, I ended up releasing something else—the one thing, in fact, that I had both always despised and thought I would always need.

I finally let go of my mother's voice inside my head!

37

WE'RE NOT IN
KANSAS ANYMORE

After I left New Mexico, my cross-country drive to New York
for my seminary ordination began with two days of gale-
force winds and torrential hydroplaning rain as my best friend
Pamela and I drove tandem in two cars across the Great Plains.
It ended a week later with me in the parking lot outside my
friend Karen's New York apartment, slumped over the steering
wheel and sobbing, wishing—like a six-year-old sent to camp
against her will—that I could click my heels and go straight
back home.

Two weeks later, Allie and I found ourselves on top of the
highest mountain in Acadia National Park in Maine, a place I
had longed to visit my whole life. Looking out at the sea and
the rolling green mountains with my sweet puppy by my side, I
literally felt on top of the world.

This has been the ebb and flow I have encountered every
day on the Way of Being Lost. Some stratospheric highs and a
few more Death Valley lows, but mostly all the liminal spaces

between high hopes and hard truths where I have been learning to wildflower myself whole.

On this road trip of intentional homelessness, I made only one commitment to myself: I vowed not to be suckered into easy answers or quick solutions. I promised to stay the course, no matter how difficult it became, no matter where it took me—inside and out.

I have come to love this quote by Samuel Beckett: "Ever tried. Ever failed. No matter. Try again. Fail again. Fail better." But I've decided it's even better when I conflate it with an old Japanese proverb: "Fall down seven. Get up eight."

When I was in my thirties, I decided to learn how to snowboard. As a rank beginner, I signed up for a group lesson—which turned out to be me and five boys under seven. I had always heard that snowboarding had a quick learning curve. It does—if you're under seven. Those boys got it within the first lesson. All I did was fall. A couple of times I fell so hard that I finally understood why cartoon characters saw stars! My head went black with sparkling lights as all 5'11" of me crashed down onto the hard-packed snow. Undeterred, I decided a few weeks later to try another lesson—this time without the seven-year-old boys.

On my first run, I still felt discouraged. I fell again and again. On the next lift ride up, I complained about falling to my 19-year-old instructor. He turned to me and quietly delivered a piece of wisdom I have never forgotten.

"Duuuude," he drawled. "You've got to get over the idea that falling is bad."

I looked at him and burst out laughing in pure joy and utter relief as I instantly remembered the fun of being a kid and falling… when falling meant adventure, freedom, and fearlessness. I knew this unlikely guru had just given me a spiritual mantra for life.

Now, whenever I'm struggling with fears that seem overwhelming, I say to myself: *Duuuuude, you've got to get over the idea that falling is bad. Ever tried. Ever failed. No matter. Fail again. Fail better. Fall down seven. Get up eight.*

Living on the road has not only taught me how to fail and fall and then get up and do it all over again, it has also taught me how to have fun doing it. Living on the road has helped me see that joy cometh not only in the sunny hopeful mornings of our lives, but even in our darkest hours when our only joy practice is, in the words of W. H. Auden, to stagger onward rejoicing. Rejoicing that darkness, too, is rejoicing—rejoicing that whatever I need to hear, whatever the next steps may be, they will come. Rejoicing that the monsters of my imagination are never the truth of my story, that I will always come home and find joy waiting with open arms.

For so many years, fear had me convinced that I would never be able to show up to my best life as my truest self and do something that made a contribution to our world. Now, in the moments of my brightest light, I feel like my wildest dreams were merely the palest intimations of the freedom, authenticity, and joy I now feel.

When I first began the journey back to my truest self, my father's joy had been my compass. Now I was walking beside him. No more following in his footsteps, walking in his shadow. By living on the road and finding the courage every day to encounter what my favorite poet, Rainer Maria Rilke, describes as "the most strange, the most singular, and the most inexplicable," I was finally stepping into the joy of living as my truest self.

On my Way of Being Lost, I have driven through towns so poor that the buildings sagged from the weight of their own abandonment, yet their streets were lined with flowering tulip trees raining their pink petals on every path. On my Way of Being Lost, I have watched white birds whirl and spin in a sunset sky over a sewage plant brimming with the stench of hot summer nights. On my Way of Being Lost, I have filled my gas tank surrounded by burly guys in pickup trucks with shotgun racks and have ended up chatting with them about our mutual love of football. I have seen rescued tigers in their forever-home sanctuaries and wept as the dead deer by the side of the road became too numerous to count. I have seen all the brokenness and beauty of the world in the most strange and singular and inexplicable of ways.

⁓

I have written this book all over the world—in the homes of friends and in hotel rooms; on construction sites and in coffee shops; on planes, on trains, and while sitting on my tailgate in a parking lot. But by far the most memorable place was at the Sea Ranch in Northern California.

From the time I began the book, I felt called to go there. When I was a little girl, it was the place my mother had adored most in the whole wide world. A place my mother, my father, and I had often visited together. I remembered it as one of the most beautiful places I have ever been. I had not been back since my parents' divorce.

The whole time I was writing my father's biography during the late 1990s, I worried so much about how it would affect my mother. She was still alive, and I didn't want to cause her pain. My fear about her reaction to the book colored my whole writing experience.

As it became clear just how much of this book was going to be about healing my relationship with my mother, I felt that fear surface again. Although she was no longer alive, I felt pressure to write my mother right. When I thought about the Sea Ranch, I had the idea that if I could connect with her in a place she had loved so much, I would find some ease.

There was only one little problem—I couldn't find anyplace to stay that I could afford. I was about to give up when I got the nudge. *Look one more time,* that still, small voice whispered. I did, and what I found was a miracle: the perfect place at the more than perfect price in the perfect location—right on the bluffs overlooking the Pacific. So I headed to the Sea Ranch.

This architecturally planned community of minimalist modernist homes built in weathered wood was calling me. It is a truly interspiritual place where man and nature meet in such harmony. The quiet homes do not impose themselves upon the glorious rocky coastline. There are miles of trails with superb panoramas and secluded spots for just sitting and seeing. Growing up surrounded by the weight of all my mother's stuff, I always felt the Sea Ranch as a breath of fresh air. In the evolution of my own design aesthetic, the Sea Ranch was the first place that made any sense.

Like me, my mother loved being outside. Like me, she loved the long view—vistas that stretch for miles. Like me, she adored animals, birds, trees, the ocean. She felt so safe at the Sea Ranch that she let me wander out on my own there. As a kid who lived with an armed security guard, I loved the freedom of hiking on the bluffs, watching the waves, riding horses, and seeing the birds and the harbor seals. So when I returned as an adult, I thought that being at the Sea Ranch would be my opportunity to connect with my mother in a place we both had loved.

On my journey of forgiveness, I had let go of so many of my old stories about my mother. I had excavated, exhumed, and erased so many old memories. I'd come to see her through the compassionate light of forgiveness in all her humanness. But there was one thing I hadn't done. I hadn't loved my mother. Just. Loved. Her.

I came to the Sea Ranch to love my mother. And, finally, I did.

When I got to my rented house on the first night, I opened the door and realized that it had not been remodeled since the early 1970s. I was immediately flooded with *déjà vu*—even wondering if my family might have rented this exact home eons ago.

The memories returned of all the sweet, quiet times the three of us had had there. That's when it clicked: My memories weren't just of my mother and me. My mother and father and I had all been there together.

I had always thought that the Sea Ranch was a strange place for my museum-going, urbane, always busy father to enjoy. But when I opened the shades my first morning back and looked out at the Pacific stretching to the distant horizon, I realized why he, too, had loved it there. My father adored being at the ocean as well. It was the one place where he stopped being a workaholic and was fully present to himself.

We had come back to the Sea Ranch over and over again as a family because it was a place where we could all find joy together. Surrounded by the kind of beauty to which all three of us so deeply resonated, isolated from the rest of the world, we had been truly happy there.

⌒

During my first week, a series of massive storms lashed the Northern California coast. The winds howled, huge waves pounded the cliffs, rains flooded the coastal route, giant trees crashed down outside my door and blocked the road. We lost power for almost a day.

Every time the rain broke, Allie and I rushed outside to hike the bluffs.

My mother always told me that her favorite thing in the world to do was to watch waves—waiting for that infinitesimal moment when one is about to crest before it begins to crash. "That's the most beautiful moment in the world," she'd said to me once.

Walking the bluffs, as I watched fifteen-foot waves rolling like thunder toward me, I treasured that sweet shared knowing of her I still carry in my heart. As I witnessed each wave crest and then crash, my mother and I continued our lifelong conversation about the beauty of the waves. I experienced every wave intensely, as though I were seeing them for two.

Then I got it. I saw what she had always seen.

As waves begin to swell and build to a crest, there is a brief instant of anticipation as the wave is at its height—right before the wave crashes down and the water curls back upon itself and rejoins the ocean again. In that exquisite moment of power and release, there is a transparent luminescence where the water belies its illusion of solidity, and you can see right through the wave to the light beyond. The sky and the water are all one.

All One.

This was the Love I had been waiting my whole life to really feel. By being crumbled, releasing the stoniest parts of my own heart, being willing to keep trying something different, and surrendering over and over again—the love that had always existed between my mother, my father, and me had finally wildflowered whole.

38

MY YELLOW
BRICK ROAD

At the end of *The Wizard of Oz,* Dorothy finally understood the fundamental truth we all eventually come to learn on The Way of Being Lost: "If I ever go looking for my heart's desire again, I won't look any further than my own back yard. Because if it isn't there, I never really lost it to begin with."

The Way of Being Lost is everyone's journey back to the back yards of our own hearts. We only embark on it when we are finally ready and willing to rid ourselves of the road maps of our false selves and recalibrate our compass to the true north of the true heart of our truest selves, which we never really lost to begin with.

The Way of Being Lost can be your worst nightmare or your most cherished dream. It's your choice. It can be a forested path of fear that circles round and round on itself, or a wide-open yellow brick road on a sunny day leading to your desired destination. Usually it's a little of both. Mostly the Way of Being Lost is everyplace in between—the ultimate threshold, a lifelong liminal space of learning.

On the Way of Being Lost, we *will* be lost. Sometimes being lost will be scary as shit. Sometimes being lost will be our most glorious adventure. We will leave behind the baggage we no longer wish to carry and then find that we need less and less anyway. Sometimes what we lose will feel like it breaks our hearts. Other times we will realize that we have lost something we never even wanted in the first place.

On the Way of Being Lost, we will be found, too—by friends old and new along the way, by thoughts that we never knew we had, by ideas that fill us with wonder, by new intentions we never imagined possible. In fact everything is possible the moment we become willing to show up to our own lives and just be. We are all traveling this way, simply by being alive. We just don't know it—or don't want to know it. We have all bought into the world's agenda—that life is about winning, gaining, accumulating. It's only when we finally become willing to cut loose from all that has not served us and elect to go where we have always wanted that we can find who we have always been. Certain twisted monsters will always bar our paths, but that's when we get going best, glad to be lost, learning how real it is here on earth, again and again.

Over the past decade, I have logged hundreds of thousands of miles on the road. If I have a choice between flying and driving to a job, I drive. I have come to realize that I need to move to think, move to pray, move to feel, to believe, to be, and to live. Movement is my meditation. My church is the road. My pew the driver's seat. The radio my choir. Every intersection becomes a threshold into another territory of Spirit. God is always in my beloved back roads, as are my fellow parishioners—the birds, the deer, the gas station attendants, and the diner waitresses. The little girl who mapped her world grew up into a woman who needs to move to understand her own life.

As much as I enjoy my time spent on the road, I would be lying if I said that it was all pure bliss. I have experienced long tedious stretches—days that went by so slowly I felt as though I were driving backwards. I have experienced fear and loneliness as well as joy. But it has been my life on the road that has taught me what I have needed to know.

Whenever I find myself disheartened on my journey, I always find a back road where I can reconnect in deep communion with myself and the world around me in what I have come to think of as my monk's cell on wheels.

I have learned so many lessons on this road trip of my life. I have experienced excitement and ennui, freedom and fear, the bustle and the boredom. I have driven too fast, too far, and too long. I have lingered in places I should have never visited. But I have always learned the most whenever I seem to have lost my way.

At first getting lost freaked me out—especially on a back road. I would panic: What if I end up someplace unsafe? Then I'd get pissed off at myself: What an idiot I am not to stay on the main roads. Finally I'd feel anxious: Damn, now I won't get there until after dark!

Each time I got lost, I witnessed this same pattern: fear, judgment, anxiety. Instead of trying to fix myself by frantically searching for the nearest highway, however, I made myself stay on the Way of Being Lost. When I did, I realized that pretty soon all those voices in my head faded away, replaced by the pure and simple delight in being right wherever I was.

Now I consciously incorporate driving the back roads into my joy practice as a glorious invitation to release all my timetables, checkpoints, and even the maps that are supposed to show me the "right way."

One of the hardest parts about spending long stretches on the road is falling into the trap of future-thinking. I've been a lifelong planner. I always thought planning would assuage my stress about the much-too-much I always seem to have on my plate.

At last I've learned this fundamental truth: The more we think about what's ahead of us, the more we worry. When we realize that right here, right now, right where we are, everything is fine, then our shoulders lower, our chest relaxes, and we can remember how to breathe. When we are anxious, it's always because we are tarring the future with the brush of our past experiences. As Eckhart Tolle reminds us: "Stress is caused by being *here* but wanting to be *there*." The key is to stay in the now.

That means learning to find joy wherever I am, even—and especially—if I am freaked out because where I am is miles away from where I thought I was supposed to be.

⌒

I have lived more of the past seven years on the road than off. It's a way of living that some people envy and others know they could never tolerate. On the road, I have found far more joy than sorrow, far more love than fear. But mostly I have found the places in between where I have begun to wildflower myself whole. By choosing to live in a way that has felt true to me, I finally learned not only to live with myself, but even to love myself a little bit more.

And by letting go of my old routine, one of the first things I lost ended up being the one and only thing I had actually ever wanted to lose. Before I began my joy practice, I always ran perpetually late. "Toria Time," as my friends, employees, and colleagues wryly dubbed it, ran as a general rule about 10 to 20 minutes later than a normal clock.

I hated myself for being late. Over the years, I was told how rude it was, how disrespectful. I knew that, of course, but the self-loathing I felt about my perpetual tardiness only made my lateness worse. I never had any success in breaking my most-hated habit.

Over the years I had gotten speeding tickets, run red lights, left my dog in the back of the car in the heat, and even blown out an engine in an effort not to be late. I had made everyone I loved madder than hell at me, and I even almost lost a few jobs. None of that ever made even the slightest dent in my lateness. No matter what I tried, I always ran late. The later I ran, the more I hated myself.

Paradoxically, because I always felt late, I never took my time. Yet no matter how much I hurried, I always arrived late. On a road trip, sometimes I would drive for 10 to 12 hours straight, waiting to pee until I had to get gas in order to assuage the taskmaster who runs the perpetual clock and calendar in my head. She is not very nice: She may have made me good at my job, but hers is a lousy way to live. Even though I did what she asked, still I ran late. We were like an old married couple, bickering in an endless cycle of bitter recrimination.

Within the first half year of my joy practice, however, I finally realized why I was always late. I was like that rebellious child who made poor choices standing up to what she felt were the unfair demands of her parent. Being late was me flipping the bird at my tyrannical inner timekeeper, who said there was no time for fun. Being late became this weird liminal space between duty and obligation in which I tried to reclaim my own life. But all being late made me was more late and more pissed off at myself for being late.

The brilliant truth I discovered is that once you stop trying to live up to the expectations of a false self, you can't be late. I learned this completely counterintuitively—by discovering how to take my time. A few weeks after posting my first Daily Practice of Joy blog, I drove from Denver to Dallas. I'd been working all weekend, and I got a late start that day. When I pulled out onto the highway, part of me said, *Take the Interstate and get there as fast as you can.* But the other part of me said, *Stick with the plan. Practice joy.*

So I did. I turned off the Interstate. When I drive the back roads, I see the glory of this planet—the antelope playing, the wildflowers by the side of the road, the thunderheads building in the distance over the mesas. When I drive the back roads, everybody waves and smiles. It's perfectly clear I'm not from there. But they still wave, and I always wave back. Because on the back roads, we all understand we're one human family.

Long stretches of open road aren't all beauty and ecstasy though. That night, as dusk fell somewhere between Denver and

Amarillo, I could see huge black clouds forming in the distance. It occurred to me that I should have checked for tornado warnings. Having been stuck in two Texas Panhandle ice storms, I knew to take their weather seriously. The radar indicated heavy storm cells coming in from the west. It didn't look promising. With darkness setting in and two hours of two-lane roads ahead, fear started to infiltrate my thoughts with all its what-ifs and you-should-haves. My shoulders crept up around my ears, and I began berating myself for my decision to take my time and not follow the main roads.

That's when it happened. A weird light flickered in the distance. Suddenly the clouds opened up and a huge shaft of red pierced through, straight down to the ground. I've always joked about wanting a burning bush—that clear sign from the Divine that tells you you're on the right path. This was pretty darn close. I'd never seen anything like it. It was huge, it was red, and it was bright. A giant shaft of vibrant crimson light that glowed for about ten minutes.

When it faded, the rain came. Two hours of a hard and steady downpour on rough roads in a pitch-black night. But from that moment on, whenever the thought came that I had been crazy to take the back roads, that I could have been at my destination already, I didn't listen. I'd had my burning bush. The back roads were where I was meant to be.

I arrived at my stop for the night not the least bit exhausted from my long day and its rain-drenched finale. Underneath all those habitual voices of fear, I had felt that peace of knowing we are always exactly where we are meant to be.

When I got to my client's house the next day, she said, "You know, I thought you were going to look haggard with the schedule you've been keeping and your long drive. But you don't. You look great."

It's joy, I told her. Joy changes everything.

Creating my daily practice of joy eradicated a lifetime habit of lateness because I had been late my whole life to a very important date—a date with my true self. No wonder I hated myself so much! Once I showed up to her instead of to that testy timekeeper in my head, once I learned how to make time for what I loved instead of feeling indignant that all I did was work, I no longer needed to resent other people's schedules. By showing up to joy, I finally showed up on time to my truest self.

If living on the Way of Being Lost could heal that most hated of lifelong habits, I knew it could heal anything.

39

A Horse of a Different Color

On a night flight over the North Atlantic a few years ago, I found myself looking out the window at the starry night, my heart beating out of my chest in terror. It had been a smooth flight—it was my life that felt turbulent. I longed to feel peace. So I began to pray, as I have through all the other dark nights and bumpy rides of my life.

That's when it happened. I couldn't tell you now whether I was asleep or awake or both.

I heard: *There is no me. There is only We.*

I felt those were the most beautiful words I had ever heard.

I felt the sweet assurance of their simple truth.

I felt the baggage of a lifetime of trying to be "me" just dissipate.

I felt free, fully loved and fully loving, totally connected, whole.

In feeling truly one with everyone and everything, I finally felt the peace that passeth all earthly understanding. Then I watched myself float out of the plane window and slip away into the stars.

When I opened my eyes, the sun was coming up and a song was rising in my heart. For days I walked through Europe as though on air. Some part of me had flown out the window into that starry night sky, yet never had I felt so present in my own life.

I had traveled halfway around the world to come home to the Truth: There is no separate self; there is only Us.

⌒

I spent so much of my life wondering why I couldn't show up to my best life as my truest self. I both wanted to be and feared that I was a horse of a different color. On that plane ride, I caught a glimpse of the unifying Truth that sets us all free.

These are the unlikely but inevitable glimpses of eternity that keep us on the Way of Being Lost. These are the true touchstones of healing to which we return over and over again to reassure ourselves with the law of Love. We find them out a window or in the smile of a little child, through the beloved gaze of our pet or among a field of wildflowers. We hear them in the lyrics to a song or on the wings of a bird.

Slowly but surely, we begin to trust that, whenever we feel the most lost, we are about to be found by the all-embracing Oneness of Love.

40

There's No Place
Like Home

I stumbled into the Way of Being Lost when my deep longing to contribute something meaningful and healing to the world led me back to the disturbed soil of my life. There, in the threshold spaces between two territories of spirits—fear and forgiveness, joy and joy kills, old stories and new narratives—I finally found my way.

We all long to come home to our truest selves. This begins the very moment we begin to listen to our false selves instead of trusting our truths. We may experience that longing in countless ways—as longing for home, for love, for conversations we can no longer have, for chances missed, for false assurances, for safety nets, for one right answer, for companionship, for a do-over, for ease, for creativity, for validation, for achievement, for success, for hope, for faith, for peace of mind. But all that we are really longing for is to live in the truth of our own hearts.

For most of my life, however, I believed that longing had a pot of gold at the end of its rainbow, that longing ended in ownership—of another person who would make me feel loved, an experience that would make me feel special, stuff that would make me feel safe, creative output that would make me feel as though I had lived up to my childhood potential, service to others that would prove I had lived a life of meaning.

So often I also longed for forgiveness, for absolution, for release. I longed to hear my mother's voice tell me that she loved me just as I am. I longed to hear my father's voice tell me he was sorry that he had left, but that he would never leave now. I longed to hear my own loving voice tell me my own loving truth.

On the Way of Being Lost, I finally realized that all I was ever longing for was Love. With the Big L.

We spend our whole lives longing for someone we already are. We long for love to make ourselves feel whole, when in fact, Love has always been loving us from the inside out. *We* are the incarnation of Love in human form, and when we make peace with our longing, we realize that we have always belonged—in Love.

I learned this by walking the Way of Being Lost.

⁓

When I travel, I am always happiest halfway between wherever I have come from and wherever I am going. That is the bliss of longing. Longing is the catalyst for every change that brings healing. Longing is the place where the hope for our future meets the regrets for our past. Longing is the faith that we will all eventually return home to Love. Longing is the beautifully disturbed soil wherein we bloom ourselves back whole.

In this beautiful unknown of the in-between, Love will always shepherd us back to our truest selves. Love can never rest until we come home to our own hearts. Eventually we all come to recognize that what we have been looking for can never really be lost at all.

Once we are willing to release our most cherished identities, we realize they were never really true in the first place. When we open up our hearts, we know who we have always been. When we are willing to crumble, we always bloom. When we speak our stories in truth, we write ourselves whole. When we live as our truest selves, we help heal the world.

There is no me. There is only us.

There is no lost. There is only found.

There is no lack. There is only Love.

This is the beautiful but bumpy, healing but hard, radical but redemptive Way of Being Lost on which we will all finally companion one another home to Love.

And so it is.

Vaya con Dios.

Buen camino.

May the road rise up to meet you on your own Way of Being Lost.

ACKNOWLEDGMENTS

Writing can often feel like a solitary act. That is an illusion. Like everything in life, it takes a village to co-create a book. That has felt even more true during this road trip of intentional homelessness. Thanks to my glorious global village, I was never without a roof over my head, food on my plate, or love on the other end of the line. Which is to say, I could never have written this book without the myriad manifestations of generosity, encouragement, and inspiration shown to me by Carol Wright, Daniela and Gene Anderson, Greg Dove, Jamie Hammond, Todd Christensen, Sarah Douglas, Nancy Cintron, Gay Block, Cynthia Lucius, Peter Fuller, Patricia Bernard, Martina Navratilova, Izzy & Trey, Kim & Richard White, David Bruson, Melissa Etheridge, Aaron Lea, Bill Diamond, Robert Taylor, Dawn Nieto & Bob Gouy, Richelle Steyn, Anne Lazenby, Brigid Beckman, Renee Mercuri, Sheryl Dougherty, Jody Price, Hollis Walker, JoAnn Sabatini, Perdita Finn, Robin Winning, Jody Levine, Gail Larson, Carly Pollack, Rebecca Campbell, Lesley Riley, Tess Ayers and Jane Anderson, and Rachel Hollander.

ACKNOWLEDGMENTS

My deepest heartfelt thanks go out to my heart tribes—OSIS Class of 2016, my Living School Cluster and the worldwide community of horror fans. And for their wisdom, guidance, and many kindnesses, so much love and gratitude to Rev. Diane Berke, Rev. David Wallace, Rev. Franne Demetrician, Rev. Bob Demetrician, Rev. Joyce Lichtenstein, Rev. Sue Koehler-Arsenault, Rev. Lucinda Olson, and Rev. Robin Lane.

I am particularly grateful to Cari Jackson for helping me dive into the wreck and see all the treasures that prevail.

And, as is true of every area of my life over the past quarter-century, I could not have faced down the challenges presented by this epic road trip without the steadfast, generous, and loving spiritual guidance and support of Pamela Phinney.

To my wonderful Airbnb and HomeAway hosts, as well as to the horror con organizers and helpers, schools and organizations who have invited me to speak and have welcomed me to your cities and events, thank you for making this road trip possible.

Thank you to the readers of my Daily Practice of Joy blog, who have joined me on this journey and shared their own joys and sorrows.

A special thank-you to Tracy Lopez—my right-hand and dear friend for over fifteen years. I literally could not have done any of this without her incredible kindness, ongoing support, strong back, and bemused tolerance for all of my idiosyncrasies!

There are two people whose loving presence in my life gives me the courage to stick with this creative journey every single day—my original Cyn and my big brother Barrett.

ACKNOWLEDGMENTS

Everyone needs a best friend. Mine is Pamela Thompson, who always reminds me to lean, listen, laugh and love. And then laugh some more.

Without the incredible Mary Wright, this book, this me, this road trip, this way of being lost might never have come to fruition.

And without Karen Osit listening, reading and re-reading, cheerleading, having faith, and loving me, these past two years would not have been possible.

To the team behind this book:

Thank you Cynthia Cannell—for encouraging me to figure out what it was I really wanted to write, and for being patient while I did.

Thank you Nan Satter—for guiding the early steps of this journey.

Thank you Nora Rawn—for helping me see the bigger picture.

Thank you Katy Koontz—for one of the most interesting spiritual conversations of my life, for laughter, for curse words, for guidance, and for your joy-filled wisdom.

But mostly, thank you Jennifer Feldman—for believing in me, this road trip, and the larger message of this book. I am grateful every single day for our ongoing dialogue and this creative collaboration.

Last but very definitely not least: Although they will never be able to read these words, I hope that Jack, Nina, and Allie know that their four-legged, tail-wagging love has been one of the greatest gifts of my life.